P 944-3178
D 944-1771

2020

20

INTERACTIONS

5

JACK HOPE   MARIAN SMALL

Consultants

Valeen Chow
Ralph Connelly
Larry Elchuck
Peggy Hill
Alexander Norrie
Deborah Tempest
Stella Tossell

ESL Consultant

Wendy McDonell

GINN

Ginn Publishing Canada Inc.

ISBN 0-7702-2364-8
C94053

PROGRAM MANAGER

Shirley Barrett

EDITORS

Janice Nixon
Mary Reeve
David MacDonald

ART/DESIGN

Sandi Meland Cherun/Word & Image Design Studio

ILLUSTRATORS

Steve Attoe
John Etheridge
Linda Hendry
Dan Hobbs
Tina Holdcroft
Vesna Krstanovich
Renée Mansfield
Mike Martchenko
Louise Phillips
Jules Prud'homme
Scot Ritchie
Sami Suomalainen
Daniel Sylvestre

ACKNOWLEDGEMENTS

Acknowledgement is hereby made for kind permission to reprint the following material:
Excerpt from THE DARK by Robert Munsch. Text copyright © 1979 by Robert Munsch. Illustrations copyright © 1979 by Sami Suomalainen. Reprinted by permission of Annick Press. Printed in 1979, revised in 1984. "Overdues" text and art by Shel Silverstein from A LIGHT IN THE ATTIC by Shel Silverstein.Copyright © 1981 by Evil Eye Music, Inc. Reprinted by permission of HarperCollins Publishers. "If the World Were a Village of 1000 People" by Donella H. Meadows. From THE OLD FARMER'S ALMANAC 1992 by Yankee Publishing Inc. Copyright © 1992 by Yankee Publishing Inc. Reprinted by permission of Random House, Inc. Excerpt from THE HALF-BIRTHDAY PARTY by Charlotte Pomerantz. Text copyright © 1984 by Charlotte Pomerantz. Illustrations copyright © 1984 by DyAnne DiSalvo-Ryan. Reprinted by permission of Clarion Books/Houghton Mifflin Co. All rights reserved. Excerpt from THE LION'S SHARE from AESOP'S FABLES selected and adapted by Louis Untermeyer, illustrated by A. and M. Provensen © 1971 Western Publishing Company, Inc. Used by permission. Excerpt from MATTHEW AND THE MIDNIGHT MONEY VAN by Allen Morgan. Text copyright © 1987 by Allen Morgan. Illustrations copyright © 1987 by Michael Martchenko. Reprinted by permission of Annick Press. Excerpt from CLOUDY WITH A CHANCE OF MEATBALLS by Judi Barrett and Ron Barrett. Text copyright © 1978 by Judi Barrett. Drawings copyright © 1978 Ron Barrett. Reprinted with the permission of Atheneum Publishers, an imprint of Macmillan Publishing Company. Illustration from THE TURN ABOUT, LOOK ABOUT, THINK ABOUT BOOK by Beau Gardner. Copyright © 1980 by Beau Gardner. Reprinted by permission of Lothrop, Lee & Shepard Books, a division of William Morrow & Company, Inc.

Every reasonable precaution has been taken to trace the owners of copyrighted material and to make due acknowledgement. Any omission will be gladly rectified in future editions.

PHOTOGRAPHS

page 144, Comstock/Malak; page 174, Comstock/M. Stuckey; page 179 left, Comstock/Eric Hayes; page 179 right, Comstock/H. Armstrong Roberts/M. Koene; page 182, Comstock/William Marin Jr.

Product photos pages 49–237 by Tom McCrae

All other photos by Ray Boudreau

Printed and bound in Canada
ABCDEFGH 2000 99876543

Contents

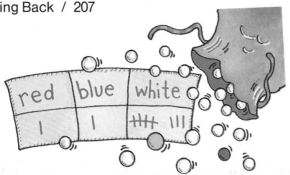

Investigating Our School

This school has 23 classrooms. How many students do you think it has?
About how many school buses would be needed for all the students in
this school to go on a field trip?
Would your school need more or fewer buses?

WHAT Do Schedules Tell Us?

Fiona studies her class schedule.

Room 15	Monday	Tuesday	Wednesday	Thursday	Friday
8:30-9:00	French	→	→	→	→
9:00-10:00	Language Arts	→	→	→	→
10:00-10:30	Phys. Ed.	Music	Phys. Ed.	Music	Language Arts
10:30-10:45	Break				
10:45-11:45	Math	→	→	→	→
11:45-12:45	Lunch				
12:45-1:00	Silent Reading	→	→	→	→
1:00-2:00	Environmental Studies	→	→	→	→
2:00-3:00	Creative Writing/ Drama	Library	Health	Art	Creative Writing/ Drama

1. How many hours is Fiona at school each day? each week?

2. How many hours of French does Fiona have each week? Estimate how many hours of French she has in the school year.

3. In one week, Fiona spends five times as many hours on math as on art. How many times as many hours does she spend on math as on French?

2

4. How much time is free time each day? About what fraction of the school day is free time?

Work in a group.

5. Use your class schedule. Compare it to Fiona's schedule. How are they the same? How are they different? How many hours do you spend at school each day? each week? each year?

6. Estimate what fraction of the school week you spend on any three subjects.

7. Draw a graph to show the number of hours spent each week on each subject in your schedule.
Draw another graph to show the number of hours you would like to spend on each subject each week.
How are the graphs different?
How are they alike?

8. Why do you think that in some schools the principal makes up class schedules for music, physical education, art, and library?

9. Make up questions about your schedule for your classmates to answer.

Did You Know...?

Schools in Moncton sometimes have to close because of winter storms.

▶ One school is closed for ten storm days. Is this more or less than 0.1 of the school year? How do you know?

WHAT's in a Floor Plan?

Caitlin and Tai drew a floor plan of their classroom and a floor plan of the school.

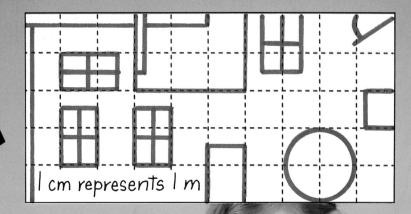

I cm represents I m

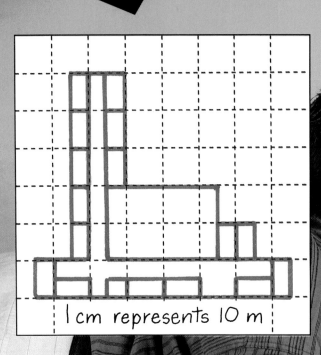

I cm represents 10 m

1. Which floor plan is for the classroom? the school? How can you tell?

2. How are the floor plans alike? different?

3. Which floor plan has the **scale** 1 cm represents 1 m?
   What do you think this means?
   What is the scale on the other floor plan? Explain what this means.

4. About how many teacher's desks would it take to cover the floor of the classroom?

5. About what fraction of the area of the whole school is the classroom?

Work in a group.

6. Discuss how to make a floor plan of your classroom. Decide
   · what measurements you need
   · what tools you need
   · what scale to use
   Draw the floor plan on grid paper.

7. Draw the desks, tables, and other furniture on grid paper. Use the same scale as the floor plan.
   Cut out the furniture pieces and place them on the floor plan of your classroom.

   Estimate what fraction of the floor area of your classroom is covered by furniture.

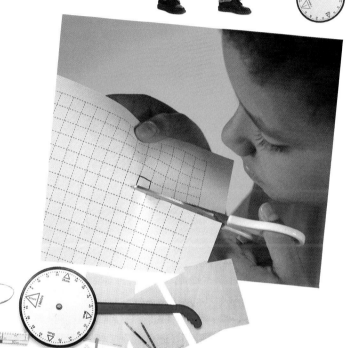

8. Work with another group to make a floor plan of your school.
   Describe how you made decisions about what measurements, tools, and scales to use in your group.
   Describe any problems you had in making the floor plan.

9. Using the floor plan of your school, find the shortest route from your classroom to an exit. Why is this important to know?

10. Which room in your school holds the most students?
    Will it hold all of the people in your school?

Did you know...?

A school in India once had an enrolment of 12 350 students.

▶ How many students are in your school? About how many times as many students were there in the school in India? Estimate the number of classrooms in that school.

5

Where Does Your School Rank?

Find out about the enrolment of other schools nearby. Is your school one of the biggest, smallest, or in the middle?

Searching the Past

How many teachers have taught at your school since it opened? How many principals has it had? In what year did it have the most students?

Fundraising

How much money would each student in the school have to raise for the school to buy
- 50 library books?
- a microscope?
- a VCR?
- a computer?
- a gym set for the playground?

Counting Students

Find out how many elementary students there are in your area.

About what fraction of the total population of your area is this?

How Far Away?

How many times do you have to walk around your school to go farther than 10 km? How many times do you have to walk up and down the halls to go the same distance?

Make up your OWN investigation. Then post it on the bulletin board for others to try.

One school raised enough money to cover the gym floor with coins. What information do you need to figure out how much money that would be?

It takes 800 children holding hands to go around a school.
How could you decide if the school is a large one or a small one? Explain.

Describe three measurements that tell something about your school.

What information would you gather to find out if your school is average?

Why might you disagree with this statement?

There are 12 classrooms in the school, so each classroom is $\frac{1}{12}$ of the area of the school.

What else would you like to know about your school? Describe what you would do to find out.

Extending

▼ Show 5 different ways to arrange 48 chairs in equal rows.

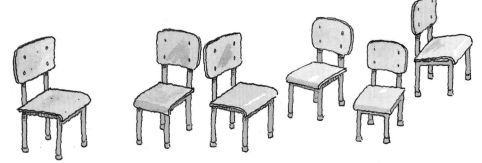

Write an addition sentence and the related multiplication sentence for this. ▶

▼ How many bars of soap might be packed in this box? Explain.

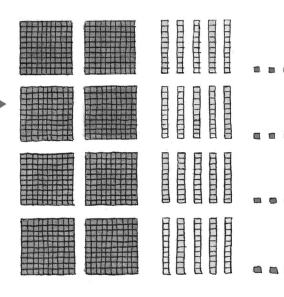

Multiplication

▼ What might this table be describing?

Distance Travelled

Time (hours)	1	2	3	4
Distance (kilometres)	90	180	270	360

How can you use the table to find the distance travelled in 5 hours?   in 6.5 hours?

◄ Think about all the times you ate yesterday.
About how many plates, bowls, knives, forks, spoons, and glasses did you use?
Estimate how many of these things are washed in one month for your meals.

9

Start with 99. Try to get to 100 by only adding 11s and subtracting 7s.

Arranging Mail Boxes

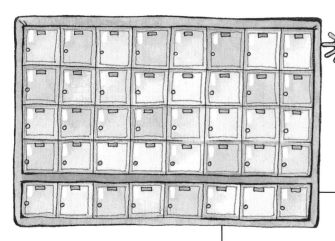

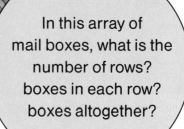

In this array of mail boxes, what is the number of rows? boxes in each row? boxes altogether?

Explain how each sentence shows the number of mail boxes.

$5 \times 8 = 40$ $8 \times 5 = 40$ $4 \times 8 + 8 = 40$

 factors   product

Work with a partner.

Use connecting cubes or grid paper.

1. Show a different rectangular array of 40 boxes.
   Write two multiplication sentences for it.

2. How many boxes are in each rectangular array?
   6 rows of 5 boxes
   7 rows of 4 boxes
   8 rows of 8 boxes

3. How many rectangular arrays of 17 boxes can you make? What other numbers of boxes less than 50 form exactly this number of rectangular arrays?

4. How many boxes are in each rectangular array if one more row is added to each?

9 rows of 10 boxes
4 rows of 25 boxes
7 rows of 5 boxes

5. Tell how the first number of boxes can help you find the second number of boxes.

5 rows of 6 = 30 boxes
6 rows of 6 = [?]

4 rows of 8 = 32 boxes
4 rows of 7 = [?]

8 rows of 20 = 160 boxes
16 rows of 20 = [?]

6. Three pieces of mail like these are placed in each of these empty mail boxes. How many pieces of mail are there altogether?

7. Create and solve a problem about an equal number of pieces of mail being placed in a rectangular array of boxes.

8. 35 boxes are in a rectangular array. If there was one less row, how many boxes might there be?

9. 56 boxes are in a rectangular array. If there was one more row, how many boxes might there be?

10. Find examples of other things in rectangular arrays. Tell how to use multiplication to find the number of things in all.

The tallest man who ever lived was 272 cm tall. Estimate and then check whether he could walk upright through your classroom doorway.
How much taller than you was he?

Eating Shadows

Jule Ann found a little, dark thing in the cookie jar. The small dark thing ate Jule Ann's shadow and got a little bigger. It ate her mother's shadow and got a little bigger. It ate the toaster's shadow and got even bigger.

"I think it's a dark," said Jule Ann.

By this time the dark was as big as the toaster.

from *The Dark* by Robert N. Munsch

The Dark grew about 1 toaster high when it ate 3 shadows.
Suppose the Dark always grows at the same rate.
How many shadows would it have to eat to be 2 toasters high?
10 toasters high?

Work in a group.

1. Complete a table like this.

Toasters high	1	2	3	?	5	6	?	?	?	10
Shadows eaten	3	?	?	12	?	?	?	?	?	?

Explain how to find the number of shadows eaten by the Dark if you know how many toasters high it is.

2. About how many centimetres high is a toaster?
Complete a table like this.

Shadows eaten	1	2	3	?	?	?	?	?	?	10
Centimetres high	?	?	?	?	?	?	?	?	?	?

Explain how to find the height in centimetres of the Dark if you know how many shadows it has eaten.

3. Estimate how many centimetres high the Dark will be after eating 30 shadows.

4. Estimate how many shadows the Dark must eat to be as high as a house.

5. Suppose the Dark grew at different rates. Copy and complete the table for each rate.

Toasters high	1	2	3	4	5	6	7	8	9	10
Shadows eaten	4	?	?	?	?	24	?	?	?	40

Toasters high	1	2	3	4	5	6	7	8	9	10
Shadows eaten	?	18	?	?	?	?	?	72	?	?

Toasters high	1	2	3	4	5	6	7	8	9	10
Shadows eaten	?	?	?	?	?	6	?	?	9	?

Toasters high	1	2	3	4	5	6	7	8	9	10
Shadows eaten	?	?	?	24	?	?	?	48	?	?

In each table, how are the numbers in each pair related?

6. In which table did the Dark grow the fastest? the slowest? Explain.

7. We can describe 1 toaster high for every 3 shadows eaten as a **ratio** 1 to 3 or 1 : 3. Write a ratio for each table.

8. Explain this bar graph. What would be the heights of the next three bars?

Examine the graph and your *Centimetres high* table from Problem 2. In which is the Dark growing faster? Explain.

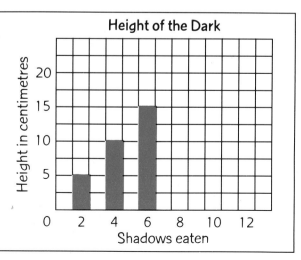

13

This shape shows 1. Show $3\frac{1}{2}$ in three different ways.

Creating Names

Finding number combinations

About how many different super-character names do you think could be created by choosing one word from each list— 20 or 50 or 100?

Stupendous   Woman
Colossal   Man
Titanic   Boy
Invisible   Girl
Micro   Dog
Transformer
Lightning
Rapid

Noam and Lois are finding how many different names can be created.

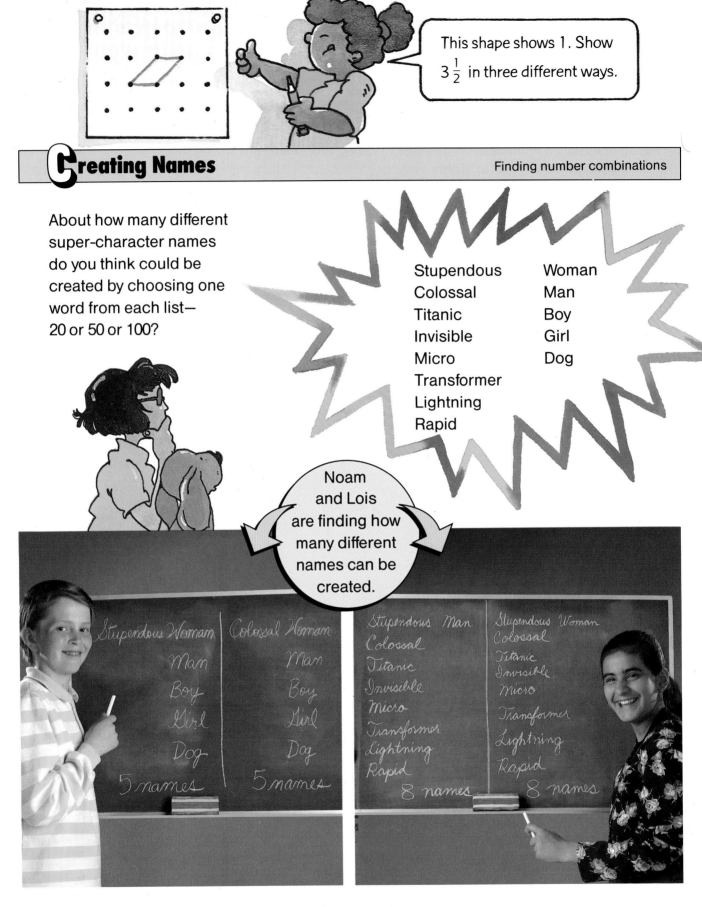

Explain each student's method.
Finish their work. Was your estimate close?

1. Explain how multiplication could be used to find the number of names.

14

2. Add a word to the first list. How many more names can be created? Why? Write a multiplication sentence to show the total number of names that can be created.

3. Add a word to the second list. How many names can be created using this list and the first list with its extra word? Write a multiplication sentence.

4. How many words might be in each list to make each number of super-character names?

   · 64
   · an even number
   · an odd number
   · between 50 and 60
   · greater than 100

5. By using the list below you can create 3-word names like Mighty Stupendous Woman. How many 3-word names can be created using this list and the two original lists? Write a multiplication sentence.

Mighty
Thundering
Dynamic
Invincible

6. Add two words to the new list in Problem 5. Write a multiplication sentence to show the number of 3-word names that can be made using this list and the two original lists.

7. How many different names can be made using the first and last names in your group? your class?

ODD SUMS

What do you notice about the sums in this pattern?

1 + 3
1 + 3 + 5
1 + 3 + 5 + 7
1 + 3 + 5 + 7 + 9

Write the addition that shows the product of 12 and 12.

List a few of your favorite main courses, desserts, and drinks. How many different meals (main course, dessert, and drink) can you form using the favorites you listed?

100 BEAN SALAD

A 100 bean salad is made with kidney beans and string bean pieces. It has 3 times as many string bean pieces as kidney beans. How many of each type of bean are used?

PLOTTING FACTORS

The numbers in the ordered pair (4, 6) multiply to give a product of 24.

Plot all the ordered pairs that have 24 as the product of the numbers. Describe the shape made by the dots. Plot the factors of 36 and then of 48. What do you notice about each shape?

TRAVELLING ANTS

Three ants leave the corner of a centimetre grid and walk continuously in different routes. One always walks 1 cm right and 2 cm up. Another always walks 2 cm right and 4 cm up. The third always walks 2 cm right and 1 cm up. Do their paths ever cross? Explain.

Make up other problems. Post them on the bulletin board for your classmates to solve.

16

Find two ways to continue this pattern.
5, 25, . . .

Rearranging Marching Bands

By marching in place, 6 rows of 15 band players become 3 groups of 30.

What other equal groups are possible for 90 band players?

Work in a group.

Draw diagrams. Use grid paper if you wish.

1. Show each band. Rearrange each into equal groups in different ways. Write a multiplication sentence for each way.

   8 × 25   15 × 16   12 × 50

2. Find 3 different ways to rearrange 16 rows of 25 players into equal groups. Which ways are most helpful for finding the number of players in the band?

3. For which is it easiest to find the number of players? Why? Which can you find in your head?

   7 rows of 37   8 rows of 15   12 rows of 50

4. The largest marching band has 4524 members. Find two different ways to rearrange this band into equal groups.

17

What two consecutive page numbers in this book have a sum of 357? a product of 342?

Going to the Bank

Multiplying multiples of ten

Joel is depositing seven $20 bills and four $50 bills. He counts. Then he checks by multiplying.

Complete Joel's work for four $50 bills.

Work in a group.

Use play money.

1. Find the amount of each deposit.

8 × $10   9 × $20   7 × $50   9 × $100

2. Complete each pattern. Make up a similar multiplication pattern.

6 × $10	7 × $4	9 × $2
6 × $100	7 × $40	9 × $20
6 × $1000	7 × $400	9 × $200
6 × $10 000	7 × $4000	9 × $2000

3. Show how the first deposit helps you find the others.

7 × $10 = $70	5 × $10 = $50
7 × $20	5 × $20
7 × $50	5 × $200

4. Roll a die to find the number of each bill to deposit. Then find the total of the deposit.

? × $2
? × $5
? × $10
? × $20
? × $50
? × $100

5. Which bills when counted or multiplied always have totals that end in zero?

6. Joel deposited $240 of the same type of bills. How many bills might he have deposited?

How old are people three times as old as you? How old will they be when you are as old as they are now?

Doing Estimation Experiments

About how many breaths do you take in a day? To find out, Ralph and Laurie did an experiment.

1 minute is up.

16 times in 1 minute
60 minutes in 1 hour
24 hours in 1 day

Ralph estimates $16 \times 60 \times 24$.	Laurie estimates $16 \times 60 \times 24$.
16×60 is about 20×50	16×24 is about 16×25
$= 1000$	$= 4 \times 100$
	$= 400$

Finish their estimates.

Why does Laurie multiply 16 and 24 before multiplying by 60?

Find another way to estimate $16 \times 60 \times 24$.

Work with a partner.

Estimate and explain what you do.

1. Suppose you could snap your fingers as fast as possible from the time you arrive at school until it is time to go home. About how many times would you snap your fingers?

2. About how long would it take to print by hand one of your favorite books?

3. About how far would you walk in a month if you walked quickly for 15 minutes at lunch each school day?

If you couldn't find a calendar, how could you find the day of the week that today's date will be next year?

Counting Windows

The front wall of an 8-floor building has 19 windows on each floor.
How many windows are in the wall?

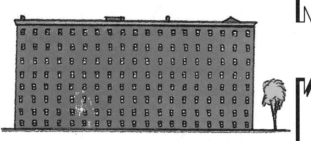

Kim uses grid paper.
She shows 8 × 20 and then removes the 20th column.

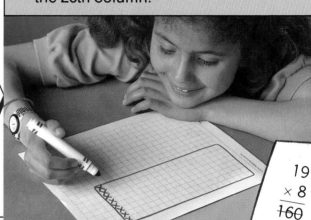

$$\begin{array}{r} 19 \\ \times\ 8 \\ \hline \cancel{160} \end{array}$$

Finish Kim's calculation.
Show another way to find the number of windows.

Work in a group.

Use grid paper or base ten blocks.

1. How does the multiplication sentence help you find each number of windows?

   8 × 50 = 400
   8 floors of 51 windows
   8 floors of 48 windows

2. Find each number of windows.

   7 floors of 29
   6 floors of 18
   5 floors of 39

3. A building has 4 floors of 19 windows on each of 4 walls. If you owned a window washing company, what would you charge to wash one window? all the windows in the building?

4. Complete each set.
   What patterns do you notice?

   | 2 × 99 |
   | 3 × 99 |
   | 4 × 99 |
   | 5 × 99 |

   | 2 × 999 |
   | 3 × 999 |
   | 4 × 999 |
   | 5 × 999 |

5. Show how to use multiplication to find the total number of windows in a large building you know.

Take Your Pick

BROKEN KEY

How could you find each product on a calculator with a broken 9 key?

7 × 99

12 × 998

9 × 555

MAKE A THOUSAND

Find pairs of numbers that have a product of 1000. Can you find any without zeros in them?

COUNTING "THE"

About how many times is the word *the* used in one of your favorite books? Tell what you did to estimate.

COIN BALANCING

The tallest single column of coins ever stacked on the edge of another coin was 205 Canadian quarters on the edge of a Canadian Olympic coin.

Estimate the height of the column. Tell what you did.

MAGIC NUMBERS

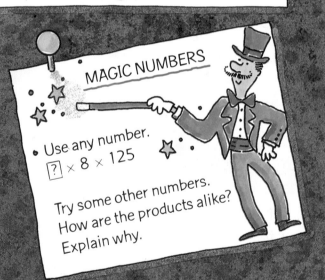

- Use any number.
  ? × 8 × 125

Try some other numbers. How are the products alike? Explain why.

Make up other problems. Post them on the bulletin board for your classmates to solve.

Use a calculator to find each product.

11 × 11   11 × 12   11 × 13   11 × 14

Describe a pattern that can help you multiply by 11.

$\mathcal{S}$elling Newspaper Ads

Katja, Simone, and some friends publish a neighborhood newspaper. They sell advertising space in it.

FOR SALE boy's bike, used 6 mos; girl's figure skates, size 4; bunk beds; men's cross-country skis; many more sports items; phone 555-0583 after 6.

Each symbol and space in an ad is considered a character. The cost of an ad depends upon the number of characters. Advertisers print their ads on grid forms.

Katja uses the grid to find the cost of this 147-character ad at 6¢ per character.

Please print clearly one character per space.

F	O	R		S	A	L	E		b	o	y	'	s		b	i	k	e	,₂₀
u	s	e	d		b		m	o	s	;		g	i	r	l	'	s		₄₀
f	i	g	u	r	e		s	k	a	t	e	s	,			s	i	z	e ₆₀
4	;		b	u	n	k		b	e	d	s	;		m	e	n	'	s	₈₀
c	r	o	s	s	-	c	o	u	n	t	r	y		s	k	i	s	;	₁₀₀
m	a	n	y		m	o	r	e		s	p	o	r	t	s		i	t	e ₁₂₀
m	s	;		p	h	o	n	e		5	5	5	-	0	5	8	3		a ₁₄₀
f	t	e	r		6	.													₁₆₀

$\Big\}$ 100 × 6¢ = 600¢

$\Big\}$ 40 × 6¢ = 240¢

$\Big\}$ 7 × 6¢ = 42¢

Finish Katja's work.

```
  H T O
      4
  1 4 7        6 × 7 pennies = 42 pennies
×     6        42 pennies = ☐4 dimes, ☐2 pennies
  ─────
     ☐2
```

```
  H T O
 ☐2 4
  1 4 7        6 × 4 dimes + 4 dimes = 28 dimes
×     6        28 dimes = ☐2 dollars, ☐8 dimes
  ─────
   ☐8 2
```

Simone uses a place value chart to find the cost of the ad.

Finish Simone's work.

Find the cost another way.

22

Model your solutions.

1. Find the cost of each of these ads at 7¢ per character.

F	O	R		S	A	L	E		B	A	B	Y		T	H	I	N	G	S₂₀
–		c	l	o	t	h	e	s	,		t	o	y	s	,		c	a₄₀	
r	r	i	a	g	e	,		e	t	c	;		m	a	t	e	r	n	i₆₀
t	y		c	l	o	t	h	e	s	;		C	a	l	l		5	5	5₈₀
–	6	8	2	1	.														100

M	O	V	I	N	G		S	A	L	E		b	e	d	s	,		d	r₂₀
e	s	s	e	r	s	,		f	r	i	d	g	e	,		f	r	e	e₄₀
z	e	r	,		w	a	s	h	e	r	,		d	r	y	e	r	,	₆₀
d	e	s	k	,		T	V	,		e	t	c	.		G	r	e	a	t₈₀
	P	r	i	c	e	s	!		1	2		M	a	p	l	e		A	v₁₀₀
e	.		S	a	t	.		9	:	3	0	–	2	.					120

2. Find the cost of each of these ads.
   - 135 characters at 6¢ per character
   - 216 characters at 4¢ per character
   - 555 characters at 5¢ per character

3. The cost of this ad at 8¢ per character is being found. Explain and finish this method.

D	A	Y		C	A	R	E		m	o	t	h	e	r		o	f		3₂₀
–	y	e	a	r		o	l	d		w	o	u	l	d		l	i	k	e₄₀
	t	o		c	a	r	e		f	o	r		2		o	t	h	e	r₆₀
	2	–	4		y	e	a	r		o	l	d	s	,		n	u	t	r₈₀
i	t	i	o	u	s		l	u	n	c	h		a	n	d		s	n	a₁₀₀
,	c	k	s	,		n	o	n	–	s	m	o	k	i	n	g		h	o	m₁₂₀
e	.		C	a	l	l		5	5	5	–	5	2	5	9	.			140

20 × 8¢ = 160¢

10 × 8¢ = 80¢   7 × 8¢ = 56¢

$$160¢$$
$$\times\ 6$$
$$\overline{960¢}$$

4. The cost of an ad is found.

$$\begin{array}{r} 2\,2 \\ 145 \\ \times\ 5 \\ \hline 725 \end{array}$$

Then the advertiser adds 10 characters. How can you find the cost without starting over?

5. Which of these ads cost less than $10? Explain what you did.
   - 245 characters at 5¢ per character
   - 129 characters at 6¢ per character
   - 345 characters at 3¢ per character

6. Find the cost of a 157-character ad at this price.
   - 5¢ per character for the first
   - 100 characters
   - 3¢ per character after the first
   - 100 characters

7. An ad had 264 characters. What price per character was charged for the cost to be about $13?

8. Make up an ad with more than 100 characters. Ask another group to set the price per character and find the cost.

9. Investigate the cost of advertising in a local paper. Find an ad and estimate its cost.

What do you need to add to 427 so that when you subtract 8216 from the sum, you get 100?

Examining Crossword Puzzles

Sergio and Lynne are finding the number of squares in this crossword puzzle by multiplying.

Sergio uses the puzzle.

Finish his work.

Make a frame.

Fill it in.

Remove the frame and find the result.

Lynne uses base ten blocks.

Explain how Lynne's model shows 23 × 12. Finish her work.

1. Make a frame with base ten blocks for each crossword puzzle.

   22 rows of 36 squares
   14 rows of 51 squares
   34 × 25

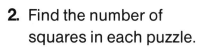

Use base ten blocks or grid paper.

2. Find the number of squares in each puzzle.	7 rows of 12 squares	12 rows of 15 squares	18 × 24

3. Show how finding the number of squares in the first puzzle helps you find the number of squares in the others.

   15 × 15 = 225   15 × 16   14 × 15   30 × 15

4. Which puzzle has the greatest number of squares?

   24 × 24   23 × 25   22 × 26

5. Find the number of rows in a square crossword puzzle with 256 squares.

6. How many rows are in a puzzle with 12 squares in a row and 156 squares in all?

7. Find a crossword puzzle in a book or newspaper. Show how to find the number of squares by multiplying.

Each letter represents a different digit. Find a solution.

```
  FOUR
+  ONE
------
  FIVE
```

Finding Fines

OVERDUES

What do I do?
What do I do?
This library book is 42
Years overdue.
I admit that it's mine
But I can't pay the fine —
Should I turn it in
Or hide it again?
What do I do?
What do I do?

from *A Light in the Attic*
by Shel Silverstein

If the fine for an overdue book is 10¢ a day, what would the fine be for the book?

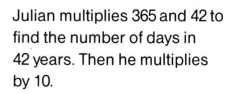

Julian and Estelle use calculators to find the fine.

Julian multiplies 365 and 42 to find the number of days in 42 years. Then he multiplies by 10.

Why does he multiply by 10?
How many dollars is 153 300¢?

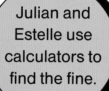

26

Estelle multiplies 365 and 10 to find the fine for 1 year. Then she multiplies by 42.

Why does she multiply by 42? Why did Estelle and Julian get the same answer?

Would you pay the fine or pay for the book?

Use a calculator.

1. Show how the fine just calculated can be used to find these fines.

   - 5¢ a day for 42 years
   - 15¢ a day for 42 years
   - 25¢ a day for 42 years
   - 30¢ a day for 84 years

2. A book costs $54.95. It is overdue 1 year and 1 day at 15¢ a day. How does the fine compare to the cost of the book?

3. At 25¢ a day, the fine for a book is $55.00. Is the book overdue more or less than 6 months?

4. Estelle thought she had multiplied $15 \times 365 \times 42$.

   The display showed 21900.

   What mistake might she have made?

5. The fine at one library doubles each day a book is overdue.

Days overdue	1	2	3	4
Fine	1¢	2¢	4¢	8¢

What is the fine for a book overdue 20 days?

6. The record for an overdue book was set when a book borrowed in 1688 was returned in 1976.
Find out the overdue fine at your library. Estimate the fine for that book.

There are lots of ways to calculate 5 × 198.
Here are some. Can you think of any more?

1. You can multiply too much and then subtract.

less

less

less

less

less

5 × 200 = 1000 less 10 → 990

5 × 198 = 990

2. You might double 5 and halve 198.

double $\overbrace{}$ half

5 × 198

10 × 99

10 × 99 = 990

5 × 198 = 990

3. You could multiply from the right and regroup.

```
 44
198
× 5
───
990
```

5 × 8 ones → 40 → 4 tens 0 ones

5 × 9 tens + 4 tens → 49 tens → 4 hundreds 9 tens

5 × 1 hundred + 4 hundreds → 9 hundreds

5 × 198 = 990

4. You could multiply in parts and add.

```
198
×  5
────
500    5 × 1 hundred
450    5 × 9 tens
 40    5 × 8 ones
────
990         5 × 198 = 990
```

Work in a group.

Show two different ways to do each multiplication.

1. 9 × 55   **2.** 5 × 298

3. 249   **4.** 129   **5.** 397
   × 6   × 4   × 3

BLAST FROM THE PAST

Try this old math problem.

25 sheep are worth 5 oxen.
5 oxen are worth 2 horses.
2 horses can be bought for $100.
What is the cost of each animal?

MAKING WISHES

On Sunday Travis was granted 3 wishes.
On Monday he used each wish to wish for 3 more wishes.
On Tuesday he used each wish to wish for 3 more wishes.
How many wishes will he have by Saturday?

CALCULATOR PATTERNS

Complete each set of 3 products.

10 × 10	20 × 20	30 × 30
9 × 11	19 × 21	29 × 31
8 × 12	18 × 22	28 × 32

What patterns do you notice?

Show how you can use a pattern to find these products without a calculator.

38 × 42   51 × 49   61 × 59   72 × 68

ANOTHER WAY

Greta multiplied 45 and 23 like this.

```
     45
   × 23
   ─────
     15
    120
    100
    800
   ─────
   1035
```

Explain her work. Check it using base 10 blocks or a grid.
Try her method for multiplying 92 and 39.

MAGIC TRICK

Think of any 3-digit number.
Multiply it by 7.
Then multiply the product by 11.
Finally, multiply that product by 13.
Try other 3-digit numbers.
What happens each time? Explain.

Make up other problems. Post them on the bulletin board for your classmates to solve.

Solving a Problem by Making an Organized List

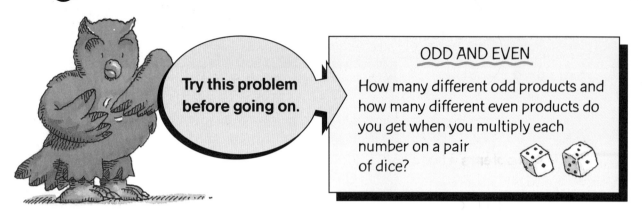

Try this problem before going on.

ODD AND EVEN

How many different odd products and how many different even products do you get when you multiply each number on a pair of dice?

Anya's group solved this problem by making an organized list.

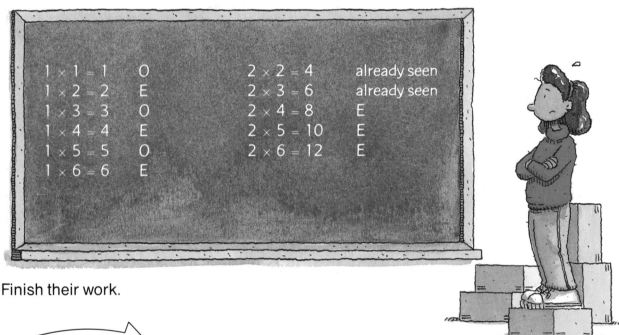

1 × 1 = 1	O	2 × 2 = 4	already seen
1 × 2 = 2	E	2 × 3 = 6	already seen
1 × 3 = 3	O	2 × 4 = 8	E
1 × 4 = 4	E	2 × 5 = 10	E
1 × 5 = 5	O	2 × 6 = 12	E
1 × 6 = 6	E		

Finish their work.

Work in a group.

Solve these problems using an organized list.

SISTERS

The sum of the ages of two sisters is greater than the product of their ages. What could their ages be?

MATH PAGES

Which page numbers in this book can be divided evenly by both 2 and 3?

MAKING CHANGE

How many ways can you make change for a dollar using dimes and nickels?

Write a problem for each of these. Then solve.

1. 8×12

2. 2×365

3. 5×1000

4. 485
$\times 7$

Solve ONLY the problems where you could use multiplication.

5. In a year, about 12 million passengers pass through Toronto's airport while 4 million pass through Calgary's. How many more passengers pass through Toronto's airport than Calgary's?

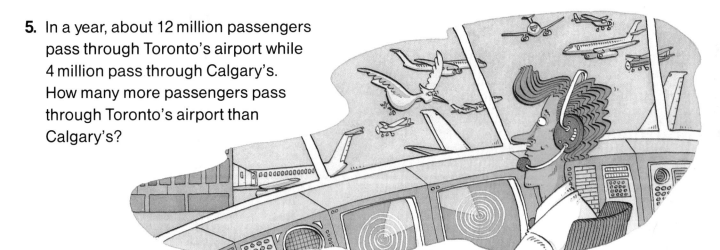

6. An Olympic runner ran a 25 km race in less than 1 hour 14 minutes. How many metres did he run?

7. How many months will it take to brush your hair 1000 times if you brush it 3 times a day?

8. What is the date 100 days from today?

9. What would you expect to pay for the larger drink?

49¢

250 mL   750 mL

10. An amateur detective kit has 5 beards, 3 wigs, and 4 noses. How many different disguises can be made using one of each?

11. A car travels 80 km in 1 hour. About how many hours will it take to travel over 1000 km?

12. A bag of popcorn costs $1.65. About how much money is needed to buy 1 bag for every 2 students in your class?

Playing Games for Practice

Play each game in a group of 2, 3, or 4.

Three in a Row

- Multiply two numbers, one from each factor list.
- If the product is on the gameboard, place a counter on that square.
- Take turns. Each player uses a different color of counters.
- The winner is the first player with 3 counters side-by-side in a row, column, or diagonal (↗ or ↘).

Factor Lists

3	4
10	5
25	6
40	20
50	80
100	200
500	1000

Example
50 × 20 = 1000
Place a counter on 1000.

250	40	50	200	100
500	320	160	400	2000
1000	3000	6000	300	240
1200	600	320	125	200
8000	10 000	800	5000	150

Greatest Product

- Spin the spinner.
- Write the digit in any square in your 4-digit by 1-digit multiplication.
- Take turns until each player has a digit in each square.
- The winner is the player with the greatest product.

Example

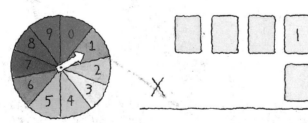

Variations:
- The winner is the player with the least product.
- Use a 2-digit by 2-digit multiplication.

RACING SNAIL

A garden snail named Verne completed a 31 cm course in a record time of 2 minutes 13 seconds.
Estimate how long it would take Verne to travel the length of your classroom.
About how many times as fast as Verne's time is your walking time?

GREATER THAN 16

How many different products greater than 16 are possible when you multiply each number on a pair of dice?

CONSECUTIVE NUMBERS PRODUCT

List any 4 consecutive numbers. Multiply the first and last numbers together. Then multiply the second and third numbers together.
Compare the products.
Try this with other sets of 4 consecutive numbers.
What do you notice?

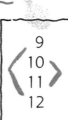

COUNTING SWALLOWS

How many times do you normally swallow when drinking a glass of water, milk, juice, or soft drink?
About how many times do you swallow when drinking in a week? in a month?

CALCULATOR PATTERN

Continue this pattern.
What do you notice?

$1 \times 90 + 21$
$12 \times 90 + 31$
$123 \times 90 + 41$
$1234 \times 90 + 51$

Make up other problems. Post them on the bulletin board for your classmates to solve.

1. How would you multiply these numbers in your head?

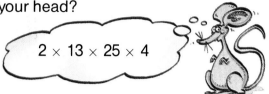

$2 \times 13 \times 25 \times 4$

2. The ratio of students wearing a watch to those not wearing one is 2 : 5. Six students are wearing a watch. How many are not?

3. How does knowing $11 \times 13 = 143$ help you find 22×13?

4. Tell how you know that 8×258 is greater than 2000 without finding the product.

5. A lunch special for $6.50 consists of
- either soup of the day or a chef's salad
- one of 4 sandwiches
- one of 3 desserts
- one of 4 drinks

How many different $6.50 lunch specials are possible?

6. The world's fastest talker can speak about 450 words in a minute. About how long will it take him to speak over 5000 words?

7. Which digits can be used in the thousands place to give a product with 4 zeros?

$5 \times \boxed{?}\,000$

8. Which are worth more— 87 six-cent stamps or 105 five-cent stamps? How much more?

9. Could there be an error? How do you know?

$\times 20 = 450$

Multiplying 3000 and 4 is as easy as multiplying 3 and 4.

What does Marian mean?

 Write about how multiplication and addition are alike. Then write about how they are different.

It's always quicker to multiply large numbers on a calculator.

Not always!

List some examples to explain what Michelle means.

$$\begin{array}{r} 299 \\ \times\ 4 \\ \hline 866 \end{array}$$

Write a note to Luke to tell him why his answer is not reasonable.

Interview two adults to find out how and when they use multiplication.

What questions do you still have about multiplication?

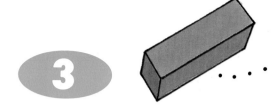

▼ Which shape is not the same as the others? How is it different?

▼ What fraction of the largest rectangle is the middle-sized one? the small one?

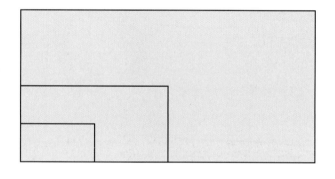

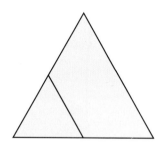

What fraction of the large triangle is the small one? ▲
Make a pattern of three triangles to show the same fractions as the rectangles.

◄ What solid could be made with this as one face?

Geometric Relationships

◀ Describe each part after the cut is made.

These imprints show all the ▶ faces of one solid.
What solid could have been used?

Name a solid that is flat on one surface but not on another. Tell three other things about it.

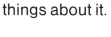

Looking at Illusions

These shapes are **congruent**.

These are not.

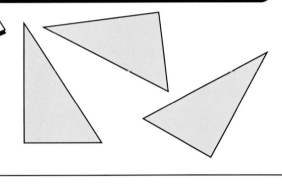

1. Draw two shapes that are congruent and two that aren't.

What do you think congruent means?

Visual illusions can make congruent shapes look like they aren't congruent.

2. Do you think the purple circles are congruent? How could you check? Describe your method.

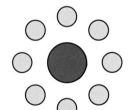
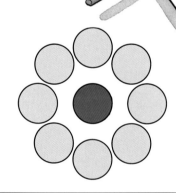

Work with a partner.

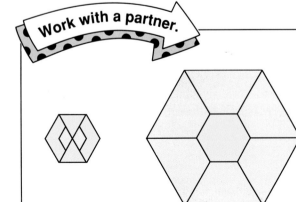

3. Do you think the yellow hexagons are congruent?
Use a different method to check.

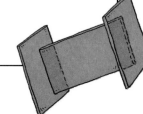

4. Do you think the blue triangles are congruent?
Use a different method to check.

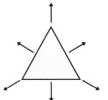

5. Use your favorite method to determine which pairs of squares are congruent. Which pairs cannot be checked easily with a Mira?

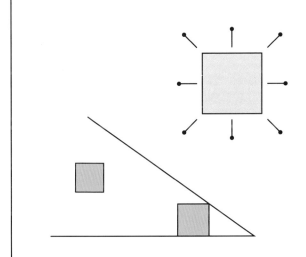

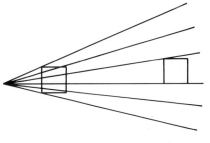

6. What is it about the diagrams that helps to create the illusions?

7. Are these characters congruent? Check.

8. Make your own visual illusion.

What might the fraction $\frac{4}{31}$ represent?

Comparing Sizes

The fronts of these boxes are **similar**.	The fronts of these aren't.

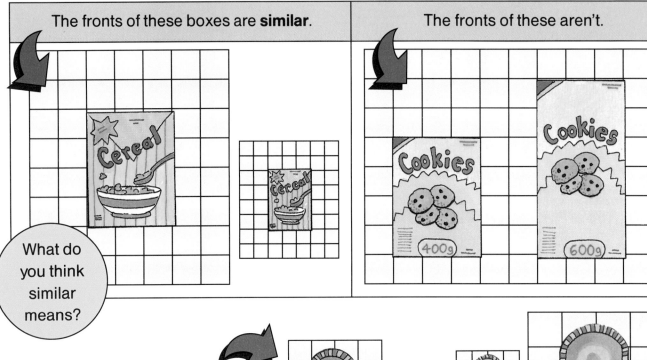

What do you think similar means?

1. Which mats are similar to the first one? How do you know?

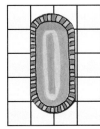 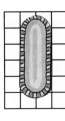 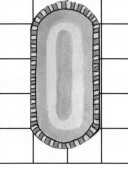

Work with a partner.

2. Use different sizes of square grids to make at least two shapes similar to each of these.

3. Are congruent shapes similar? Explain.

4. All circles are similar. What other shape can you say this about? Show why.

Place decimal points in each number so that the answers are about $50.

$992 − $491 − $11 $4225 + $155 − $712

$9992 − $199 − $3412

Planning Garden Plots

Using shapes to create number patterns

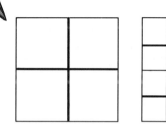

Marc drew a series of diagrams to show how a square garden could be divided into smaller plots.

How many plots are in each diagram?

How many will the next diagram show?

Use the number pattern to decide how many diagrams are needed to show more than 1000 plots.

Work with a partner.

What fraction of the whole garden is each plot?

1.

2.

3.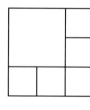

Draw diagrams using dot paper.

4. How many plots will the next two diagrams in the series show?
   Use the number pattern to decide how many diagrams are needed to show more than 50 plots.

 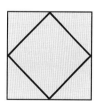 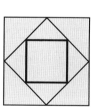

5. Make a series of at least three diagrams for dividing a garden of a different shape into smaller plots.
   Estimate at each step what fraction of the whole garden each plot is.

Take Your Pick

GETTING LARGER

The logo is enlarged by a projector. Each side is 10 times as long. What happens to the area?

CONGRUENT PARTS

Find a way to divide this triangle into four congruent parts.
Can you divide it into three congruent parts?
If so, how?

SQUARE PATTERNS

This series of shapes made with squares forms a number pattern if you count all the squares you can see.
Explain the number pattern.

Draw squares to show another number pattern.
Explain your pattern.

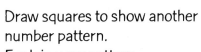   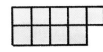

 3   **6**   **9**   **12**

TRUE OR FALSE?

Show each statement to be true or false.
- Two squares that have equal diagonals are always congruent.
- Two circles with the same circumference are always congruent.

GEOQUADS

Draw five quadrilaterals that are similar to this one.

Make up other problems. Post them on the bulletin board for your classmates to solve.

42

Each letter represents a different digit.
Why is there no solution?
FIVE + SEVEN = TWELVE

Cutting Up Desserts

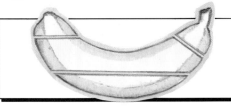

These cuts make **cross sections**.

These don't.

What do you think a cross section is?

1. Which cut gives a cross section that is a circle?
Describe the shapes of the other two cross sections.

Work in a group.

Use Plasticine to model each dessert.

2.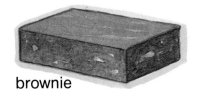
brownie

3.
ice cream

4.
cake

5.
jelly

6.
jelly roll

7.
doughnut

Make at least two different cross sections for each. Describe the shape
of each cross section.

[1], [2], and [3] form a row on a calculator.
Subtract 123 from 321.
What do you get?
What happens if you use the keys in a
different row? in a column?

Creating the Best Package

Building solids from shapes

Rosa entered a contest to create
an interesting but practical
package for selling marbles.
The package must be folded
from cardboard.

Work in a group.

1. For each package, predict what it will look like by telling
   • how many edges and vertices or corners it has
   • how many faces and curved surfaces it has
   • how many faces or curved surfaces touch at each vertex
   • the shapes of the faces or curved surfaces that touch each other
   • something that it looks like

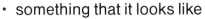

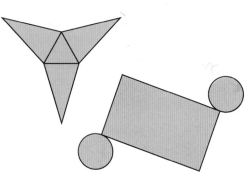

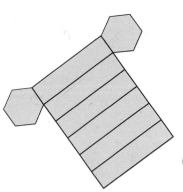

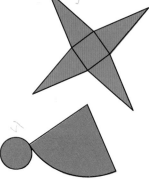

Check your predictions by using nets to make the packages.

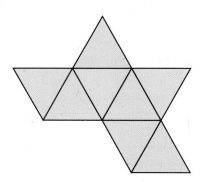

2. Make a package from a net like this.

Count faces, edges, and vertices on the package.
Why is it easy to tell how many faces it will have from its net?
Why is it hard to tell how many edges and vertices it will have from its net?

3. Make packages from nets like these.
How are the packages alike? different?

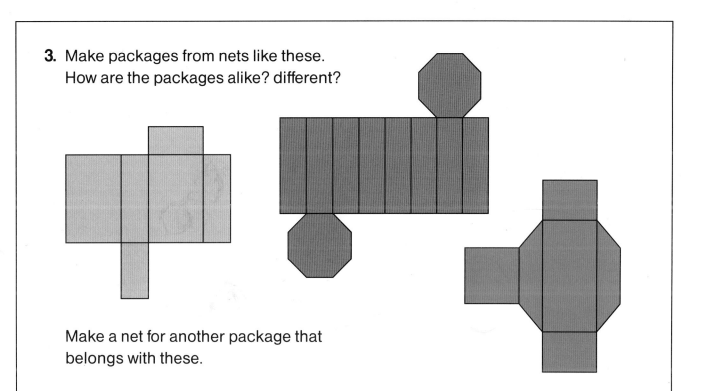

Make a net for another package that belongs with these.

4. Make packages from nets like these.
How will the packages be different? alike?

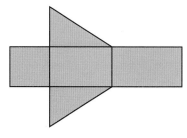

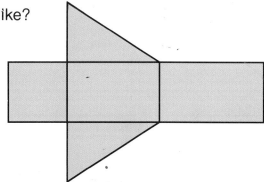

5. Is it possible to make a net for a spherical package? Explain.

6. Create a net for a package that you think could win the contest.
Why do you think it is a winner?

45

$4 + 2 = 6$ and $6 \times 1 = 6$
or $6 \div 1 = 6$
Score a point.

Throw a die three times.
Use any operations with the three numbers to try to get an answer of 6.
Score a point if you get 6. The first player to get 6 points wins.

Drawing Solids

Each shape can be the base of a prism.

Which prism would you find easiest to draw? Draw it.
Compare yours with those of others who drew the same prism.
What about the drawings make them look like prisms?

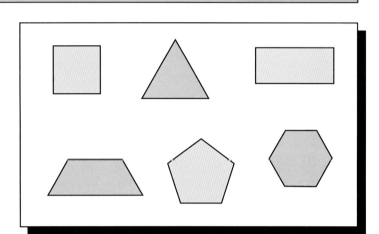

Work with a partner.

1. Try each method of drawing a triangular prism.

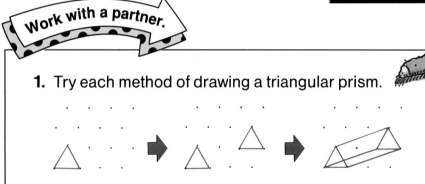

Which method do you like best? Why?

2. Use your favorite method to draw at least two other prisms.

3. Try drawing a cylinder, a cone, a pyramid, and a sphere.
Compare drawing each of these solids to drawing prisms.
What is the same? different?

46

Take Your Pick

ROTATING CUBES

Each face of the cube at the left has a different colored dot.
Which of the other cubes could show a different view of the first cube?
Draw another view of the first cube.

PYRAMID POWER

Make a pyramid like this using Plasticine.
Describe the shapes of the cross sections you can make.

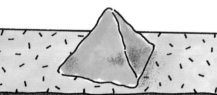

HIDDEN PARTS

What is the greatest number of faces, edges, and vertices you can see on a cube at one time?
How many of each are hidden from view?
What is the least number of each you can see at one time?
Tell how you are looking at the cube.

THREE SLICES EACH

Each solid is cut as shown.
For which solids are the cross sections congruent? similar? Explain why.

MAKE A NET

A cube has 6 faces. Draw a net of another solid with 6 faces.
What solid is it?

Make up other problems. Post them on the bulletin board for your classmates to solve.

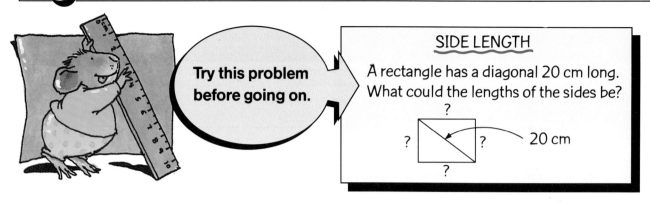

Try this problem before going on.

SIDE LENGTH

A rectangle has a diagonal 20 cm long.
What could the lengths of the sides be?

? ? 20 cm ?

Jasmine's group solved this problem by making a model.

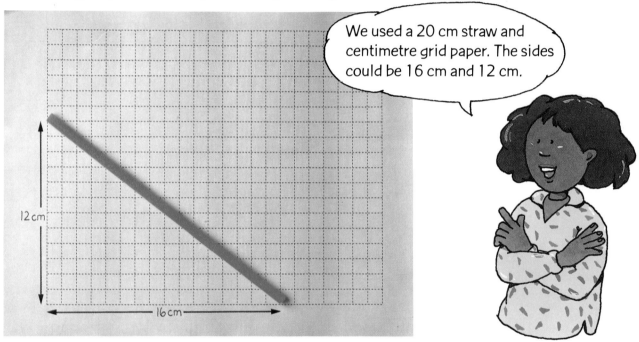

We used a 20 cm straw and centimetre grid paper. The sides could be 16 cm and 12 cm.

12 cm

16 cm

Can you find other possible solutions to the problem?

Work in a group.

Solve these problems by making a model.

HALVES

What lengths of perimeters could result when this square is folded and cut in half?

20 cm

STACKING CUBES

How could 14 cubes be stacked to have the least number of faces hidden? the greatest number of faces hidden?

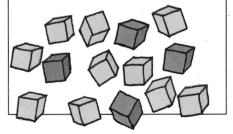

CUTTING CORNERS

The vertices are cut off a triangular prism.
How many faces, edges, and vertices are on the solid that is left?

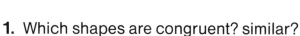

1. Which shapes are congruent? similar?

2. Which shapes could not be cross sections of a cone?

    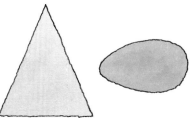

3. Make a shape congruent to this.

4. Make a shape similar to this.

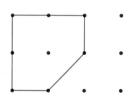

5. Draw two cylinders, one longer than the other.

6. Draw a prism with more faces than this.

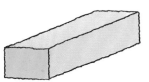

7. Describe how this pattern is made. How many sections could be in each of the next two diagrams?

 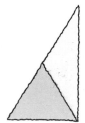 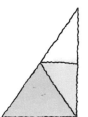

8. Describe the shapes of the cross sections when the vertices are cut off.

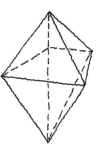

9. Show two different nets and two different cross sections of a cube.

Play each game in a group of 2, 3, or 4.

Shape Race

- Roll a die.
- Identify the shape that is that number of places along the game board.
- If the shape is
  - congruent to any pattern block, move to it and take an extra turn
  - similar to any pattern block, move to it
  - neither congruent nor similar, don't move
- Take turns.
- The first player to finish wins.

Example
The shape is similar to the trapezoid.
Move 4 spaces.

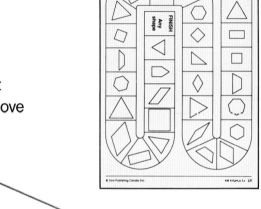

Solid Concentration

- Shuffle the cards. Place them face down in an array.
- Turn two cards face up.
- If one card is a solid and the other card shows a fact about that solid, take the cards.
- If not, turn the cards face down again.
- Take turns until no cards are left.
- The player with the most cards wins.

Example
These cards match.

4
congruent
faces

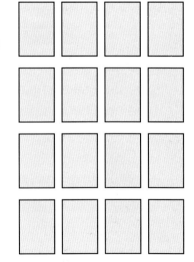

PRISMS AND PYRAMIDS

Copy and complete this table. Compare the number of faces, edges, and vertices of pyramids and prisms with the same bases.

	Pyramid			Prism		
Base	F	E	V	F	E	V
triangle	?	?	?	?	?	?
square	?	?	?	?	?	?
pentagon	?	?	?	?	?	?

What patterns do you notice?

CUBE FROM CUBES

This cube was made with connecting cubes. What is the greatest number of cubes used? the least?

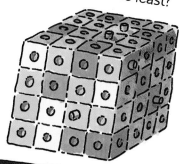

CHANGING SHAPES

How would you change the first shape in each pair to make it similar to the second one?

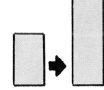 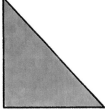 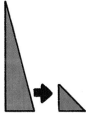

HOLEY MIDDLE

Make a cube with Plasticine. Make a cylindrical hole through the middle of it.

Describe or draw the shape of at least three different cross sections.

PYRAMID NETS

How many different nets can you make for a square pyramid?

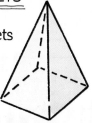

Make up other problems. Post them on the bulletin board for your classmates to solve.

1. What are three ways to check if these are congruent?

Which way would you use for these shapes? Why?

2. How long and wide a piece of paper do you need to draw a net for a cube with edges of 20 cm?

3. Two squares have diagonals the same length.
Do they have to be congruent?
What if the shapes were rectangles?
Explain.

4. Are all parallelograms similar? Explain.

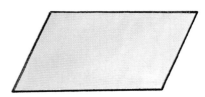

5. How is the net of a cube different from other nets you have used?

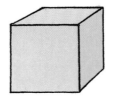

6. Each cut passes through all the previous cuts.
How many sections will there be in the next diagram in the series?

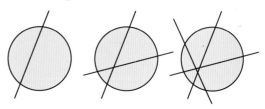

7. Describe the number pattern.
What could the 10th number be?

8. Identify three solids that could have similar cross sections.

Tell a friend why sometimes it's easy and other times it's difficult to tell if two shapes are congruent.

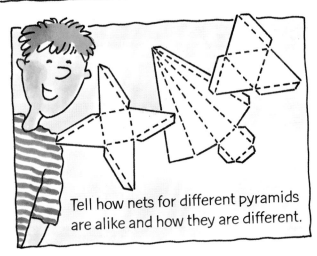

Tell how nets for different pyramids are alike and how they are different.

What did you learn about shapes that interested you the most?

Choose a solid. Write a story about living in a room the shape of that solid.

Show why all squares are similar but not all rectangles are similar.

What questions do you still have about geometric relationships?

4 Examining Fractions

◄

What fraction of the letters are used in the word RUGBY? FOOTBALL?

What fraction of all the letters are vowels?

What decimal describes the portion of all the letters that are circled?

What other fractions or decimals does this Word Search puzzle suggest?

▼ When we compare the number of green cubes in the first and second trains, we see that $\frac{3}{10} > \frac{2}{10}$.

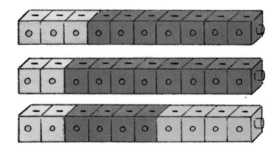

What other comparisons do the first and second trains show? Use fractions. What are you comparing?

What comparisons do the first and third trains show? Use decimals. What are you comparing?

▼ What fraction of each team are these athletes?

| basketball 5 players | baseball 9 players | hockey 6 players |

54

and Decimals

▼ About what fraction of all the students does each colored section represent?

What Is Your Favorite Fast Food?

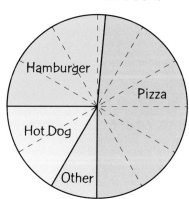

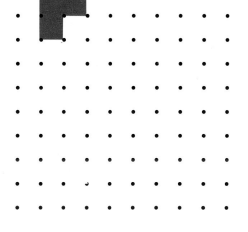

▲ This shape is $\frac{1}{2}$ of another shape.

What might the other shape be?

What if this shape was $\frac{1}{3}$ of another?

$\frac{1}{5}$ of another?

Would you use a fraction or a decimal to describe each situation? Explain.
- a length of ribbon between 16 cm and 17 cm
- the portion of a family of 10 that are adults
- the portion of your class that are girls

Write a fraction or decimal sentence to describe something about yourself.

Without doing the calculations, decide which two answers will be closest to 200. Explain your thinking.

$\frac{1}{3}$ of 700

75 + 175

425 − 189

412 ÷ 2

63 + 75 + 89 + 12

22 × 9

Using Fractions in Quilts

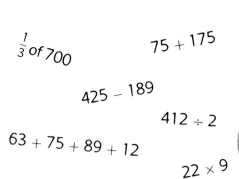

Mara is making a square patch that is $\frac{1}{4}$ blue, $\frac{1}{4}$ green, and the rest will be yellow. What is meant by $\frac{1}{4}$ blue?

What fraction of Mara's square patch will be yellow? Why?

Patchwork Designs

The shape used most often in patchwork is the square. A square patch is divided into smaller squares or triangles. The colors of the smaller shapes make a design. Sometimes the designs are given names.

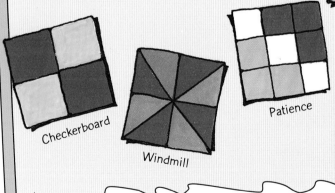

Friendship Star

Tam's Patch

Checkerboard

Windmill

Patience

Mixed Squares

Simple Star

1. Design a different square patch with the same fractions of the three colors.

2. Which of the designs are $\frac{1}{3}$ red? more than $\frac{1}{3}$ red?

3. Which of the designs show fourths? What other fractions do they show?

4. Which of the designs show thirds? What other fractions do they show?

Color and cut out square patches.

5. Make part of a quilt using 3 Patience patches in blue and yellow like this. What fraction of one patch is one square?

How many squares are blue?

Why can you say $\frac{18}{9}$ patches are blue?

Cut out and rearrange the squares to show that 2 patches are blue.

Why can you say that $\frac{18}{9} = 2$?

Describe the yellow squares two ways.

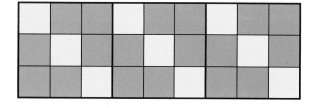

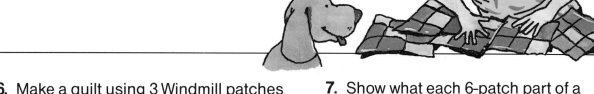

6. Make a quilt using 3 Windmill patches in blue and green.
How many eighths are blue?
Cut out and rearrange the triangles to show that 1 and 1 half patches are blue.
Describe the green triangles two ways.

7. Show what each 6-patch part of a quilt might look like.
   - 2 and 4 eighths white
     1 and 1 eighth blue
     2 and 3 eighths green
   - 1 and 1 ninth blue
     7 ninths red
     4 and 1 ninth yellow
   - 1 and 3 eighths purple
     3 eighths pink
     6 eighths yellow
     3 and 4 eighths green

For each design, how many sections are in one patch? How many sections are needed in all?

8. What is wrong?
   How would you correct it?

I have 6 patches made with 3 colors. Two patches are purple, 2 and 7 eighths are yellow, and 1 and 3 eighths are green.

9. Design a quilt and describe the colors using
   - fractions
   - whole numbers and fractions

Divide this square into 4 sets of 4 numbers. The sum of numbers in each set must be 50.

10	9	22	7
25	16	9	16
8	16	6	21
1	11	12	11

easuring Unusual Objects

In $\frac{3}{10}$, what does the 3 mean? the 10?

How do you read 0.3 m?

1. What fraction and decimal would describe the paper clip if it was longer by 1 dm?   20 cm?   1 m?   5 cm?

2. Use a fraction and a decimal to describe the length of each giant eraser as a part of a metre.

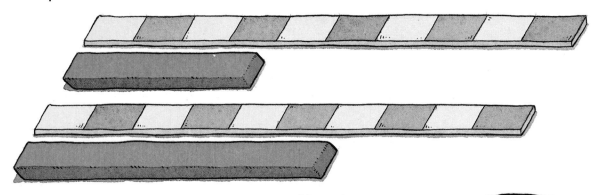

- an eraser 5 dm long
- one 82 cm long

3. Which decimal describes this running shoe — 0.5 m or 0.05 m? Tell why.

4. This giant soccer ball is 2.36 m across.
   How many centimetres across is it?

   Which way do you read 2.36 m?
   · 2 and 3 tenths, 6 hundredths of a metre
   · 2 and 36 hundredths of a metre

5. A yo-yo is 1.82 m across. How would you read this decimal?
   Is this yo-yo unusually large or unusually small?

Work with a partner.

6. Make a model of each object.
   Describe each length in centimetres
   and decimetres.
   Is each of these objects unusually
   large or unusually small?
   · a pencil 0.45 m long
   · a pancake 0.01 m across
   · a pizza 0.78 m across
   · a carrot 0.83 m long

7. Cut string to each length.
   4.23 m   1.2 m   0.32 m   0.04 m
   For each length, describe an object that is usually
   that length, and an object that isn't usually that length.

8. The length of an unusual bed is ? . ? m.
   How many centimetres long might it be?

9. A giant basket is 1 m + 7 cm + 5 dm tall.
   How tall is it in metres? decimetres? centimetres?

10. Find an unusual object at home. Measure it in metres. Bring in the
    object or a drawing with its measurements.

You have 20 counters.
All of the purple squares must hold the same number.
No square can have more than 6 counters.
What different ways could you arrange the counters?

Living in a Global Village

If The World Were A Village of 1000 People . . . by Donella H. Meadows
(for 1992)

If the world were a village of 1000 people, it would include:
  584 Asians
  124 Africans
   95 East and West Europeans
   84 Latin Americans
   55 Soviets
   52 North Americans
    6 Australians and New Zealanders

The people in the village have considerable difficulty in communicating:
  165 Mandarin speaking
   86 English speaking
   83 Hindu/Urdu speaking
   64 Spanish speaking
   58 Russian speaking
   37 Arabic speaking
  507 speaking one or more of over 200 other languages

In this village of 1000, there are:
  329 Christians
  178 Moslems
  167 non-religious
  132 Hindu
   60 Buddhists
   45 Atheists
    3 Jews
   86 all other religions

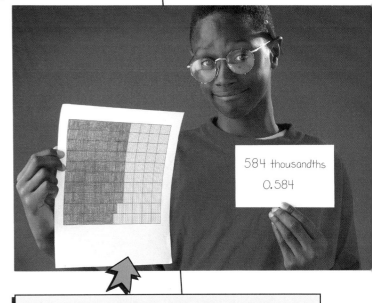

584 thousandths
0.584

Jeremy is using a grid to show the decimal part of the global village that would be Asian.
What fraction should he write?

Work with a partner.

1. Write a decimal for each group of villagers. Show each decimal on a thousandths grid.

   · Africans
   · non-Africans
   · Christians
   · Moslems
   · non-religious

60

2. Which describes the North Americans — 0.52 or 0.052? Explain.
   Show the decimal that describes the North Americans on a thousandths grid.

3. Write a decimal to describe the portion of the village that speaks each
   language. Show three of these facts on a thousandths grid.

4. Write a decimal for each of these facts about the global village.

   · 28 babies are born during the year.
   · 10 people die during the year.
   · 60 people are over 65 years old.
   · One third of the people are children.
   · Half of the children have received shots for
     diseases like measles and polio.
   · 70 people own one or more automobiles.
   · Seven people are teachers.
   · One person is a doctor.

---

5. If the article was about a village of 100 people, then the number of
   Asians would be 58.

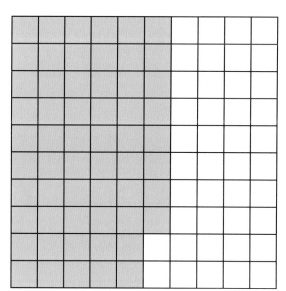

   What decimal would describe the
   Asians now?
   Compare this grid with the one showing
   the Asians in the village of 1000. How
   do the grids help you to see why 0.584
   is 58 hundredths + 4 thousandths?

---

6. What decimals would describe the
   people of other nationalities in both
   villages of 1000 and 100?
   Show one on both grids.

7. Tell how you might use a thousandths
   grid to show facts about your
   community.

LICORICE STRIPS

One strip of licorice is 0.42 m long.
How long would half of a strip be? a quarter of a strip?
Use centimetres as well as metres.

HOUSEHOLD ITEMS

What portion of Canadian households do you think owns each item? Use these decimals.

0.99	0.98	0.71
0.68	0.13	0.08

CD player   clothes dryer
microwave oven   telephone
computer   television

FRACTION PATTERNS

What would you put next in this pattern?

Create a fraction pattern of your own.

SPLIT IT UP

What fraction of the whole rectangle is each part?

MEASURING HAIR

A human hair is about 0.007 cm wide. About how many hairs placed side-by-side would measure 1 cm? 1 m?

Make up other problems. Post them on the bulletin board for your classmates to solve.

62

How could you use multiplication to find how many pennies would fit on the cover of your math book?

Watching Videos

$\frac{2}{2} = 1$

Lana says she would spend 1 h (hour) watching her favorite $\frac{1}{2}$ h video if she watched it twice.
Why did she write $\frac{2}{2} = 1$?

If she watched it three times, she would spend $\frac{3}{2}$ h or $1\frac{1}{2}$ h.
$1\frac{1}{2}$ is a **mixed number**. Why do you think it is called mixed?

Work with a partner.

Use fraction pieces. Record your answers as fractions and mixed numbers.

1. How many hours would be spent watching
a $\frac{1}{2}$ h video 9 times?   a $\frac{1}{4}$ h video 10 times?   a $\frac{1}{4}$ h video 5 times?

2. What fraction of an hour does it take to watch a 20 min (minute) video? a 10 min video? a 12 min video?
How much time would be spent watching each 8 times?

3. Juan says he could spend $3\frac{1}{3}$ h watching his favorite video.
How long might it be? How many times would he be watching it?

Draw a shape like this. Draw another line across the square in a different place. What shapes can you make?

Buying Dozens

$\frac{1}{2}$ of the doughnuts are chocolate.

$\frac{6}{12}$ of the doughnuts are chocolate.

$\frac{1}{2}$ and $\frac{6}{12}$ are **equivalent** fractions.

Why do you think they are called equivalent?

Write a pair of equivalent fractions to describe each as a fraction of the whole container.

1. blueberry muffins   bran muffins

2. vanilla cookies   chocolate cookies

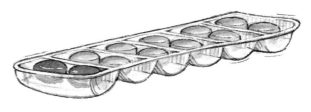

3. lemon tarts   cherry tarts

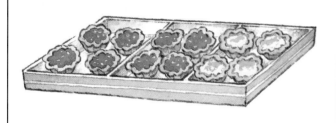

4. brown eggs   white eggs

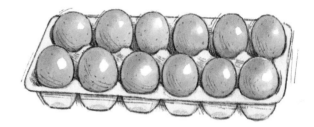

 Work with a partner.

Use egg cartons, dividing strips, and counters.

5. Show each fraction of a dozen.
Then name a fraction equivalent to it.

$\dfrac{3}{4}$ $\dfrac{5}{6}$ $\dfrac{3}{3}$ $\dfrac{4}{6}$

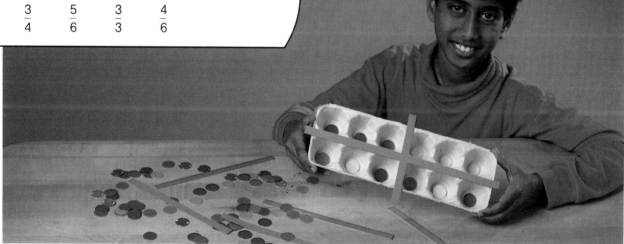

6. Show why each pair of fractions is equivalent.

$\dfrac{1}{2}$ and $\dfrac{2}{4}$ $\dfrac{1}{2}$ and $\dfrac{3}{6}$ $\dfrac{1}{4}$ and $\dfrac{3}{12}$

Compare the numerators and denominators of each pair.
What do you notice?

7. Make up and check a rule about the numerators and the denominators of equivalent fractions.

Does the rule work for $\dfrac{3}{4}$ and $\dfrac{9}{12}$?
$\dfrac{2}{4}$ and $\dfrac{3}{6}$?

8. Find three more pairs of equivalent fractions for dozens.
Why is $\dfrac{1}{5}$ not included?

9. Why is it easier to find equivalent fractions using a dozen rather than using only 11?

Irene is multiplying 36 and 15.
She thinks 36 × 10 = 360 and 5 is half of 10.
How might she use this to find 36 × 15?

Reading Survey Results

600 out of 1000 Canadian households own their own homes.

$\frac{6}{10}$ **Households Own Their Homes**

$\frac{60}{100}$ **Own Homes**

ults from

HOME OWNERSHIP
Results from Statistics Canada shows 0.600 of Canadian households own their own homes

0.6 of Canadian households own their homes

Statistics Canada results show 0.60 of households own

Canada
ership in
at the

What fractions and decimals do you see in the newspaper clippings?
Could all the clippings be about the same survey?

Tony and Helen are using hundredths grids to show that 0.6 and 0.60 are equivalent.

Color a thousandths grid and compare it with the two other grids to show that 0.600, 0.6, and 0.60 are equivalent.

1. How many of 1000 households do not own their own homes?
Describe them using three equivalent decimals.

Use hundredths and thousandths grids.

2. A survey found that 21 out of 100 Canadian households are one-person households. Do both models describe this information? Explain.

   What decimals are shown?

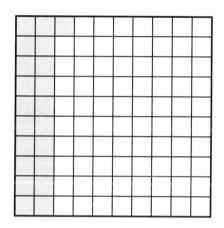
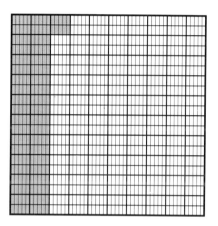

3. How many small rectangles are colored?
   Use three decimals to describe the part of the grid that is colored.

   Make up a survey result to match this data.

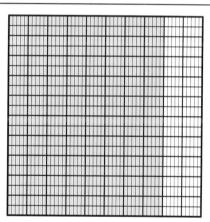

4. A survey showed that 0.673 of Canadian families have children living at home. Show this on a grid. Tell how the grid shows that 0.673 = 6 tenths + 7 hundredths + 3 thousandths.
   How might reading decimals this way help show why 0.67 = 0.670?

5. Explain why 0.45 = 0.450 but 0.45 > 0.045.

6. Survey 10 students about some aspect of their lives. What decimals would show equivalent results if you surveyed 100 students? 1000 students? Do you think your results would change if you actually surveyed 1000 students? Explain.

The outline of a shape goes through 6 squares on a 10 by 10 grid. What might the shape be?

Recycling and Returning Pop Containers

$\frac{25}{100}$, $\frac{1}{4}$, and 0.25 all describe the glass bottle portion of the box. Tell why. What decimal and fractions describe the portion that is pop cans? plastic bottles? all bottles?

1. What fractions and decimal describe the portion that is pop cans? plastic bottles? recyclable? returnable?

Work in a group.

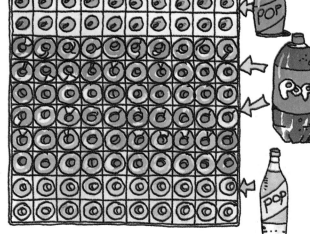

Use counters and a hundredths grid as a pop container box.

2. Show each fraction of a full box. Write an equivalent fraction and decimal.

$\frac{2}{4}$ $\frac{3}{4}$ $\frac{3}{5}$ $\frac{1}{20}$ $\frac{2}{20}$ $\frac{1}{25}$

3. Model the decimal that is closest to $\frac{1}{3}$ of a full box.

4. Show $\frac{1}{100}$ of a full box. Then imagine that 9 identical boxes are stacked under that one.
   Which of these describe how full the boxes are? Explain.

   $\frac{1}{100}$ 0.01 $\frac{10}{1000}$ 0.010

   What fractions and decimals describe the portion that is empty?

Take Your Pick

$\frac{1}{2}$ GRAPH

What labels could be added to explain how this graph shows different names for $\frac{1}{2}$? Copy the graph and show four more names for $\frac{1}{2}$.

Make a $\frac{1}{3}$ graph. How is it like the $\frac{1}{2}$ graph? How is it different?

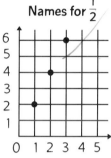

Names for $\frac{1}{2}$

RIGHT OR WRONG?

André said that $\frac{1}{4} = 0.4$. Is he right or wrong? Show why.

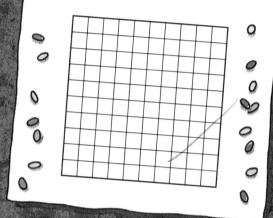

FRACTION PATTERNS

What are the next two fractions?
Is there still a pattern when the fractions are changed to mixed numbers? Explain.
Create a pattern with mixed numbers. Do the equivalent fractions also make a pattern?

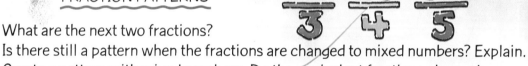

$$\frac{12}{3} \quad \frac{23}{4} \quad \frac{34}{5}$$

EIGHTHS

Use a thousandths grid to find a decimal equivalent to each fraction.

$\frac{4}{8} \quad \frac{3}{8} \quad \frac{2}{8} \quad \frac{1}{8}$

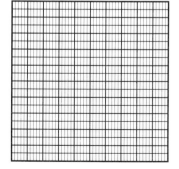

DECIMAL PATTERNS

Continue the pattern for 4 more fractions.

$\frac{1}{20} = 0.05 \qquad \frac{2}{20} = 0.10 \qquad \frac{3}{20} = 0.15$

What fraction is equivalent to 0.55?   0.75?

Make up other problems. Post them on the bulletin board for your classmates to solve.

ADAm
weinz

69

16 m

20 m

20 m

50 m

30 m

Start → 36 m

If you walk 500 m around this building, where will you end up?

Comparing Ages of Inventions

Invention	Age (in decades)
Chewing Gum	12.4
Milk Bottle	11.5
Sneaker	12.5
Sandwich	23.1
Tea Bag	8.9

Which invention is older — chewing gum or the tea bag?

Megan is using a number line.

Why do numbers farther to the right indicate greater age?

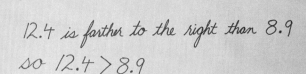

Tea Bag   Chewing Gum

0 1 2 3 4 5 6 7 8 9 10 11 12 13 14

Decades

12.4 is farther to the right than 8.9

so 12.4 > 8.9

Ken is changing decades to years. How many years is a decade?

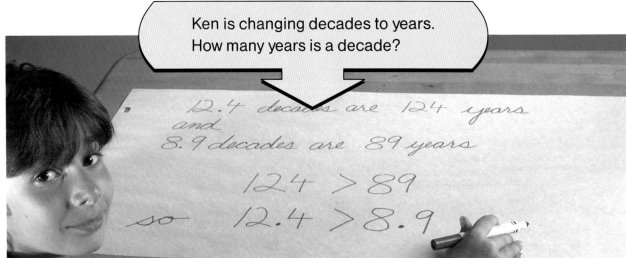

12.4 decades are 124 years
and
8.9 decades are 89 years

124 > 89

so 12.4 > 8.9

70

Ann is comparing the whole numbers.

12 > 8
so 12.4 > 8.9

How did you decide which was older?
Whose method would not work to compare the ages of chewing gum and the sneaker?
How might that student compare those ages?

Work with a partner.

1. Show all the inventions from the previous page on a number line.
   Write 3 decimal comparisons about their ages.

2. Order these inventions from most recent to oldest.
   Write 3 decimal comparisons about them.

Invention	Age (in decades)
Chocolate Chip Cookie	6.3
Playing Cards	100.7
Roller Skate	23.3
Television	6.7
Tin Can	18.1

3. How many years is a century?
   Show the ages of the inventions above in centuries.
   Write 3 decimal comparisons using the century ages.

4. How many decades old is each invention?

   Color Film   Zipper   Drinking Straw   Telephone

   0 1 2 3 4 5 6 7 8 9 10 11 12 13 14
   Decades

5. A millennium is 1000 years.
   Show the ages in the number line in millenniums.
   Write 3 decimal comparisons.

6. Describe other situations where you compare decimals.

A square pyramid is placed on each face of a cube. How many faces, edges, and vertices does the new shape have?

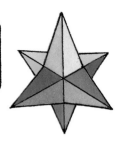

Comparing Ingredients

Many recipes use mixed numbers and fractions.

Yogurt Sauce

$2\frac{1}{2}$ cups	yogurt	625 mL
$\frac{1}{3}$ cup	sugar	75 mL
$\frac{1}{4}$ cup	orange juice	50 mL
$\frac{1}{2}$ teaspoon	lemon juice	2 mL

Measure each pair to decide which is the greater amount. Then decide how you can tell by just comparing the numbers.

1. $\frac{1}{2}$ cup butter

$1\frac{1}{4}$ cups sugar

2. $\frac{1}{4}$ cup water

$\frac{3}{4}$ cup flour

3. $\frac{1}{3}$ cup coconut

$\frac{1}{2}$ cup pecans

4. $\frac{3}{8}$ cup oil

$\frac{3}{4}$ cup sugar

Work in a group. **Use measuring cups.**

Gumdrop Nut Bread

$\frac{2}{3}$ cup sugar

$\frac{1}{3}$ cup oil

$\frac{1}{2}$ cup walnut pieces

$\frac{3}{4}$ cup gumdrops

3 cups flour

$1\frac{1}{3}$ cups milk

$\frac{1}{4}$ teaspoon salt

$\frac{1}{2}$ teaspoon vanilla

5. Tell how to use the numbers to decide which amount is greater.
- flour or milk
- sugar or oil
- oil or walnut pieces

Can you look at just the fractions for vanilla and oil to decide which amount is greater? Explain.

$\frac{1}{2} = \boxed{\frac{2}{4}}$ and $\frac{2}{4} < \frac{3}{4}$ so

6. Fred is comparing walnut pieces and gumdrops.

Which is the greater amount? Explain what he is doing and why. Use his method to compare

 $\frac{2}{3}$ and $\frac{5}{6}$ $\frac{2}{3}$ and $\frac{3}{4}$

7. Myra is comparing oil and gumdrops. Explain what she is doing and why. Compare these ingredients using Fred's method from Problem 6.
Whose method do you like better? Why? How can you compare these ingredients another way?

$\frac{1}{3} = \frac{3}{9}$ and

$\frac{3}{9} < \frac{3}{4}$ because

9ths are smaller than 4ths

so $\frac{1}{3} < \frac{3}{4}$

8. Order the amounts of gumdrop nut bread ingredients from greatest to least. Describe how you did it.

9. Order the amounts of these ingredients from least to greatest. Tell how you did it.

$2\frac{1}{3}$ cups oil

$\frac{5}{3}$ cup raisins

$\frac{2}{3}$ cup nuts

$\frac{3}{4}$ cup sugar

$\frac{3}{8}$ cup coconut

10. Why do measurements like $\frac{3}{6}$ cup and $\frac{6}{8}$ cup usually not appear in recipes?

Take Your Pick

STRING LENGTHS

By estimating, cut two pieces of string so that one is about 0.22 m longer than the other.
Then measure. How accurate were you?

DIFFERENT WAYS

Try to find at least 6 ways to use 1, 2, 3, and 4 to make this statement true.

SHARING THE EARTH

Look at an atlas. Which decimal describes the amount of the Earth taken by each land mass?

Africa
Antarctica
Eurasia
Australasia
The Americas

0.202

0.057

0.281

0.093

0.367

COMPARING FRACTIONS

In $\frac{3}{4}$, $\frac{5}{6}$, and $\frac{7}{8}$, 5 is between 3 and 7, and 6 is between 4 and 8.
Is $\frac{5}{6}$ between $\frac{3}{4}$ and $\frac{7}{8}$?

Is the second fraction between the first and the third?

- $\frac{1}{4}$, $\frac{2}{8}$, and $\frac{3}{12}$?
- $\frac{1}{3}$, $\frac{2}{8}$, and $\frac{3}{10}$?

ZERO TO FOUR

Show 6 ways to use each of the digits from 0 to 4 to make this statement true.

$$0.\boxed{?}\boxed{?} > 0.\boxed{?}\boxed{?}\boxed{?}$$

Make up other problems. Post them on the bulletin board for your classmates to solve.

74

Solving a Problem by Guessing and Testing

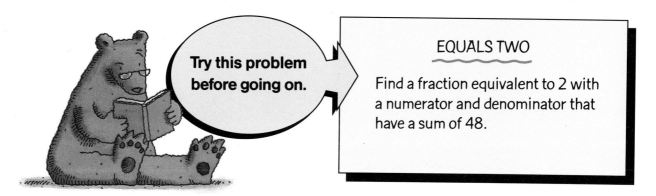

Try this problem before going on.

EQUALS TWO

Find a fraction equivalent to 2 with a numerator and denominator that have a sum of 48.

Veronica's group solved the problem by guessing and testing.

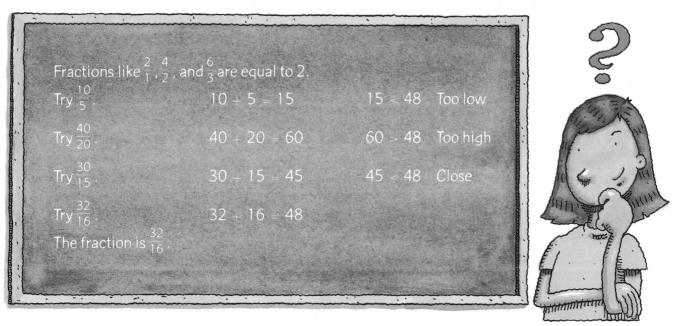

Fractions like $\frac{2}{1}$, $\frac{4}{2}$, and $\frac{6}{3}$ are equal to 2.

Try $\frac{10}{5}$. $10 + 5 = 15$ $15 < 48$ Too low

Try $\frac{40}{20}$. $40 + 20 = 60$ $60 > 48$ Too high

Try $\frac{30}{15}$. $30 + 15 = 45$ $45 < 48$ Close

Try $\frac{32}{16}$. $32 + 16 = 48$

The fraction is $\frac{32}{16}$.

What if the fraction is to be equivalent to 3?

Work in a group.

Solve these problems by guessing and testing.

SUM OF 20

Create a number so that
- the sum of its digits is 20
- the thousandths digit is greater than 7
- one digit is 3 greater than another
- the number is greater than 0.75

0.$\boxed{?}$$\boxed{?}$$\boxed{?}$

GEOBOARD FRACTIONS

A shape that touches 4 pegs is $\frac{1}{6}$ of another shape that touches 10 pegs. What do the shapes look like?

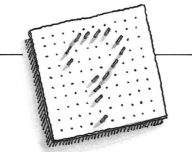

GREATER THAN

Find a rule that relates the denominators to make this statement true.

$$\frac{3}{\boxed{?}} > \frac{6}{\boxed{?}}$$

Hint: First try $\dfrac{3}{\boxed{?}} = \dfrac{6}{\boxed{?}}$

1. Use hundredths or thousandths grids to show

   0.15   0.20   0.243

2. Show each statement using models.

   $\frac{1}{2} = 0.5$ $1.25 < 1\frac{1}{3}$ $\frac{2}{3} < \frac{3}{4}$

   $3.20 = 3.200$ $2\frac{1}{3} = \frac{7}{3}$ $\frac{2}{3} = \frac{6}{9}$

3. Locate each on a number line.

   2.3   1.87 $\frac{13}{4}$ $2\frac{3}{5}$ $\frac{16}{10}$

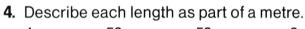

4. Describe each length as part of a metre.

   4 cm   58 cm   58 mm   3 dm   6.2 dm

Solve these problems.

5. This centipede is wearing boots on 72 of its 100 feet. Describe the portion of feet wearing boots using a decimal.

6. Patrick is 1.25 m tall. How tall is he in centimetres? decimetres? millimetres?

7. Who is the tallest? shortest? Who are closest in height?

Justin	Mabel	Anthony	Charlene	Bill
1.29 m	1.19 m	1.42 m	1.24 m	1.32 m

8. A recipe for zoo food calls for $2\frac{1}{2}$ cups of crickets, $1\frac{3}{4}$ cups meal worms, and $\frac{1}{4}$ cup of water. Will this fit in a 5-cup bowl? How can you tell?

Playing Games for Practice

Play these games in pairs.

Dicey Fractions

- Toss a die twice.
- Make a fraction using the first number tossed as the numerator and the second number as the denominator.
- Score 3 points if your fraction is greater than 2
  - 2 points if it is equal to 2
  - 1 point if it is between 1 and 2
  - 0 points if it is 1 or less
- Take turns.
- The winner is the first player to reach 15 points.

Example

$\frac{5}{2} > 2$ Score 3 points.

Decimal Show Down

- Shuffle and deal all the cards face down.
- Both players turn over the top card in their piles.
- The player with the greater decimal takes both cards.
- If the decimals are equal, both players turn over another card. The player with the greater decimal takes all 4 cards.
- Play until one player has no cards left.

Example

0.400 > 0.35

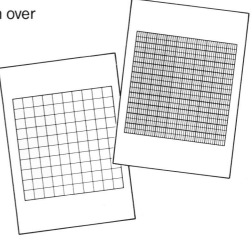

Variation: The player with the lesser decimal takes both cards.

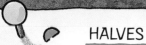

HALVES

How many fractions equivalent to $\frac{1}{2}$ are there with a 1-digit denominator? a 2-digit denominator?

FOURS

What fraction of the numbers from 1 to 1000 have more than one 4 in them? Express this as a decimal.

NAMING ODD SHAPES

What decimal is ⬡ : if ☐ : is 1? if ▭ : : is 1?

What shape is 1 if this shape is 0.5? 1.5?

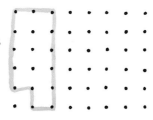

REARRANGING DIGITS

Rearrange the digits of this number to make a number that is less than it.

How many numbers can you find?

SHARING A HEXAGON

Find a way to cut the hexagonal cake to share it equally among 5 people.

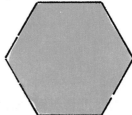

Make up other problems. Post them on the bulletin board for your classmates to solve.

1. Show 0.43 using two different models.

2. Explain why each piece is one-sixth.

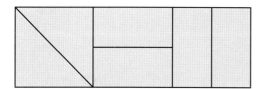

3. Use any digits to make this statement true.

   ? . ? > ? . ? ? ?

4. What happens to the size of a fraction when you
   - double both the numerator and the denominator?
   - triple the numerator and double the denominator?
   - double the numerator and triple the denominator?

5. Which is greater —
   the fraction of faces of a triangular prism that are triangles   or
   the fraction of faces of a hexagonal prism that are hexagons?

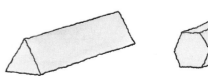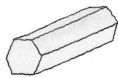

6. What are four other names for 2.25?

7. Who is right?

   This is 3 and 245 thousandths.

   This is 3 and 2 tenths, 4 hundredths, 5 thousandths.

   3.245

8. Show why $\frac{3}{5}$ is another name for $\frac{6}{10}$.
   What would be another name for $\frac{30}{50}$?

9. Change $\frac{13}{4}$ and $\frac{22}{5}$ to mixed numbers.
   Is it easier to compare them as fractions or as mixed numbers?
   Tell why.

Thinking Back

Tell a friend how you can use a number line to compare fractions and decimals.

0.234 is a lot bigger than 0.8.

Is Carlos right or wrong? Explain.

Zeros aren't needed after the decimal point to show decimals because 0.2 = 0.20 = 0.200.

Tell Sophie why she's not quite right.

Tell as many things about $\frac{1}{6}$ as you can.

APPLES 2 for .0.99¢

What is wrong with the sign? How would you correct it?

What questions do you still have about fractions and decimals?

Investigating Nutrition and Health

NUTRITION INFORMATION / APPORT NUTRITIONNEL

	Per 40 g serving cereal (175 mL, ¾ cup) / Par ration de 40 g de céréale (175 mL, ¾ tasse)	Per 40 g serving cereal with 125 mL Partly Skimmed Milk (2%) / Par ration de 40 g de céréale avec 125 mL de lait partiellement écrémé (2,0 %)	
ENERGY	130Cal 540kJ	195Cal 810kJ	ÉNERGIE
PROTEIN	3.0g	7.3g	PROTÉINES
FAT	0.4g	2.9g	MATIÈRES GRASSES
CARBOHYDRATE	32g	38g	GLUCIDES
SUGARS*	11g	18g	*SUCRES
STARCH	16g	16g	AMIDON
DIETARY FIBRE	4.6g	4.6g	FIBRES ALIMENTAIRES
SODIUM	235mg	300mg	SODIUM
POTASSIUM	240mg	440mg	POTASSIUM

1% B.F. partly skimmed milk

Fieldfresh

1% B.F. partly skimmed milk

1 litre

KEEP REFRIGERATED

an excellent source of calcium

NUTRITION INFORMATION NUTRITIONNELLE
per 250 mL serving (1 cup) / par portion de 250 mL (1 tasse)

Energy / Énergie	108 450	Cal kJ
Protein / Protéines	8.5	g
Fat / Matières grasses	2.7	g
Carbohydrate / Glucides	12	g

% RECOMMENDED DAILY INTAKE / % de L'APPORT QUOTIDIEN RECOMMANDÉ

Vitamin / Vitamine A	11%
Vitamin / Vitamine D	44%
Calcium	29%

Raisin Bran — Kellogg's — Two scoops! / Deux pelletées!

About how many servings of milk are in the milk carton?

How can you tell that about one quarter of the cereal is sugar?

What other problems can you create using this information?

Collect empty food packages and read the labels. What numbers and measurements can you find?

81

WHAT Is in Fast Food?

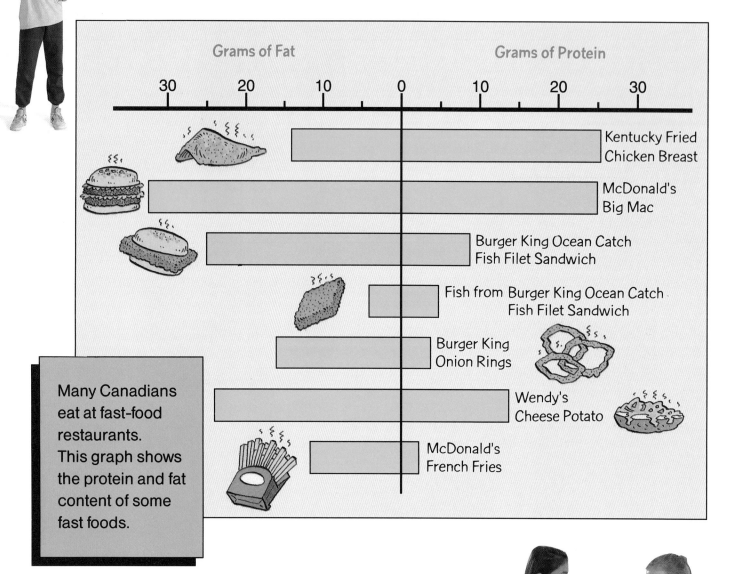

Grams of Fat   **Grams of Protein**

30   20   10   0   10   20   30

- Kentucky Fried Chicken Breast
- McDonald's Big Mac
- Burger King Ocean Catch Fish Filet Sandwich
- Fish from Burger King Ocean Catch Fish Filet Sandwich
- Burger King Onion Rings
- Wendy's Cheese Potato
- McDonald's French Fries

Many Canadians eat at fast-food restaurants. This graph shows the protein and fat content of some fast foods.

Use the graph.

1. Which foods contain more fat than protein?

2. Which food contains the most fat? the least?

3. Which food contains the most protein? the least?

4. Compare the two potato foods.
   What might explain the differences in fat and protein content?

5. Tell how you know that the average amount of fat in these foods is greater than 10 g and less than 30 g.
   What do you think the average amount of fat is?

82

6. About how much protein do you need each day? Which foods in the graph would provide one third or more of this daily requirement?

7. In the graph, the fish in a Fish Filet Sandwich has a mass of about 100 g. The same mass of fish when cooked in a microwave has about 1.0 g of fat and 19.0 g of protein.
How would a bar graph of this look different from the graph for the fish in the Fish Filet Sandwich?

The Food We Eat

Protein is essential for muscle and tissue growth, repair, and maintenance. About 0.15 of our energy should come from protein. We need about 40 g each day. Good sources of protein are meats, beans, and dairy products.

We need to eat fat for healthy skin, steady body temperature, and reserve energy. Fat is necessary for absorbing certain vitamins and is a source of essential nutrients. Most Canadians eat too much fat. We get about 0.40 of our energy from fat and we should get no more than 0.30.

8. This chart shows the amount of protein and fat in some other fast foods.

Food	Grams of Protein	Grams of Fat
Dairy Queen Hounder	16.0	36.0
Taco Bell Taco	10.0	11.0
Pizza Hut Pepperoni Pan Pizza	29.0	22.0
Wendy's Garden Salad	7.0	5.0

Make a bar graph to display this information.

9. What else would you like to know about fast foods? What can you do to find out?

Did you know...?

On an average day, Canadians eat 284 932 kg of potato chips.

▶ About how many bags of potato chips would have this mass?

WHERE Is the Sugar?

Sugar and Fibre Content of Ten Breakfast Cereals

Cereal	Grams of sugar per 30 g serving	Grams of fibre per 30 g serving	Package size in grams
Corn Flakes	2.3	0.8	400
Honey Nut Corn Flakes	9.2	0.8	525
Bran Flakes	3.3	4.4	475
Froot Loops	14.0	0.5	275
Grape Nuts	2.1	3.6	375
Shreddies	4.7	2.7	675
Marshmallow Alpha-Bits	15.0	0.8	400
Rice Krispies	2.9	0.3	350
Sugar Crisp	13.0	1.2	400
All Bran	5.3	10.0	575

Work in a group.

Use the chart.

1. Order the cereals from the greatest to least amount of sugar per serving.

2. Which cereals are about half sugar? For each cereal, about how many spoonfuls of sugar are in one serving?

3. Which cereals are about one third sugar? less than one tenth sugar?

5 g

4. The recommended daily intake of fibre is 25 to 30 g. Which cereals provide about one third of your daily fibre in each serving? more than one tenth?

5. About how many servings of Froot Loops would you need to eat to provide one third of your daily fibre?

6. About how many servings of cereal are in the package with the greatest mass? the least mass?

7. Can you tell from the names of the cereals which ones contain the greatest amounts of sugar? Explain.

8. How do you know that All Bran cereal is not all bran?

9. Each decimal describes the portion of a cereal that is sugar. Make up a name that you think best describes the sweetness of each cereal.

10. What are the fibre and sugar contents of your favorite cereal?
Can you find other cereals that contain more fibre and less sugar?

Two Scoops

About how many raisins are in each scoop? What could you do to find out? Do you think the scoops are the same size for a 60 g package?

Healthy Eating

Make up a one-day menu using *Canada's Food Guide to Healthy Eating*. How many servings should you select from each food group? Compare your menu with what you ate yesterday.

Meaty Peanuts

100 g of peanuts contains about 49 g of fat and about 24 g of protein. Estimate the amount of fat and protein in a 1.5 kg container of natural peanut butter.
Explain why peanuts are grouped with meats rather than fruits and vegetables.

Disappearing Gum

Find the mass of 5 Chiclets in a small cup. Cover the Chiclets with hot water and leave them for a few hours. Carefully drain the water out so the gum stays in. Let the cup and gum dry overnight.
Find the mass of the cup and Chiclets again.
How can you explain what you saw and measured?

Comparing Potatoes

How many servings of french fries can you make from an average potato? How much would these french fries cost at a fast-food restaurant? Compare this to the cost of the potato.

Make up your OWN investigation. Then post it on the bulletin board for others to try.

Thinking Back

What part of the chicken egg do you think is missing from the imitation egg product? Use this information to help you explain.

Poached Egg

2.8 g protein
5.1 g fat

3.5 g protein
0 g fat

Egg Substitute

6.3 g protein
0 g fat

Examine numbers and measurement units shown on food packages. Tell what you know about these numbers and units.

Tell what you notice about this chart. Investigate why calcium is an important nutrient. What foods and drinks contain calcium?

Recommended Daily Amounts of Calcium		
Age (years)	Females (mg per day)	Males (mg per day)
under 4	500	500
4-6	600	600
7-9	700	700
10-12	1000	900
13-15	800	1100
16-18	700	900
19-49	700	800
over 50	800	800

Source: Health and Welfare Canada

smooth

crunchy

Peanut Butter Preferences of Canadians

Conduct a survey of peanut butter preferences in your class or school. Write about what you found out.

What else would you like to know about nutrition and health? Describe what you would do to find out.

Extending

◀ Tell how 4 friends can share 7 sandwiches.
What fraction will each get?

▼ Complete each division.

$3\overline{)4}$ $3\overline{)7}$ $3\overline{)10}$ $3\overline{)13}$ $3\overline{)16}$

What patterns do you notice? What division would you write next?

▼ Ravi is dividing 240 by 6.

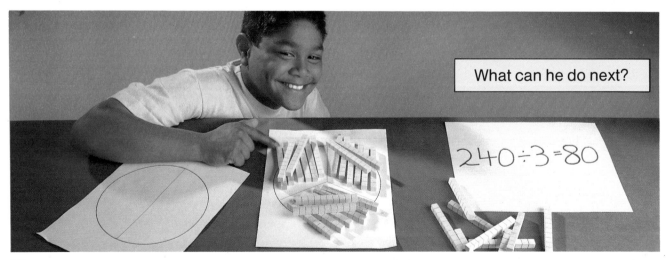

What can he do next?

240 ÷ 3 = 80

Division

▲ Show how to fold a 100 cm tape to find these parts.

$\frac{1}{2}$ of 100 $\frac{1}{4}$ of 100 $\frac{1}{8}$ of 100

◀ A man roller-skated 1488 km
in just over 9 days.
How can these calculations
help you estimate how far
he skated each day?

$9 \times 100 = 900$
$9 \times 200 = 1800$

▼ Use one of these facts in a
division problem.

365 days in 1 year
1000 m in 1 km
500 sheets in a package
210 staples in a strip
250 mL in a carton

Describe two ways to find how much time has passed between **9:45 AM** and **2:40 PM**

Displaying Collections

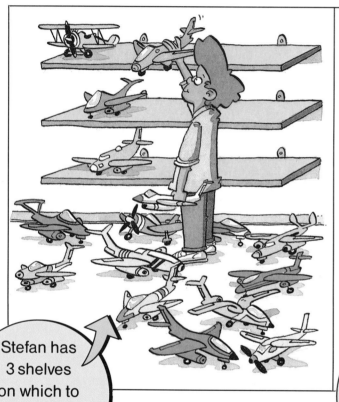

Stefan has 3 shelves on which to display 16 model planes.

Can he display them with an equal number on each shelf? Explain. How many planes will be on each shelf?

Jackie is displaying 16 model planes with 3 on each shelf.

How many shelves will she use to display them? Why?

Explain each number in Stefan's division sentence.

Explain each number in Jackie's division sentence.

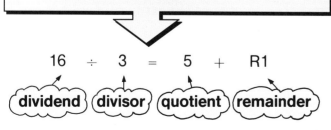

16 ÷ 3 = 5 + R1

dividend **divisor** **quotient** **remainder**

16 ÷ 3 = 5 + R1

How are the two division methods different? the same?

Model each solution by sharing or making equal groups of counters.

1. Which number of planes can be displayed with the same number of them on each of Stefan's 3 shelves?

    18   24   28   37

    How many will be on each shelf?

2. How many shelves will Jackie use to display each number of planes with 3 on each shelf?

    17   22   33   39

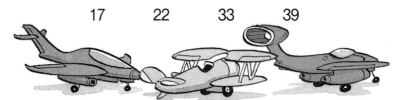

3. Make up a division problem about planes and 3 shelves using this division sentence.

    $23 \div 3 = 7 + R2$

4. Make up a division problem about planes with 3 on each shelf using this division sentence.

$$\begin{array}{r} 9 + R2 \\ 3\overline{)29} \end{array}$$

---

5. Six hockey cards can be displayed on one page.
   How many pages are needed to display 37 cards? 42 cards? 57 cards? Write a division sentence for each.

6. A hockey card display has between 30 and 40 cards. If each page has exactly 6 cards, how many cards are displayed?

---

7. Stamps are displayed with the same number on a page. There are no stamps left over when either 6 or 8 pages are used. How many stamps might be displayed?

8. Stamps are displayed with the same number on a page. There is 1 stamp left over when 3, 4, or 5 pages are used. How many stamps might be displayed?

9. Make up a division problem about something that people like to display in books or on shelves.

Double your age in years. Then multiply the result by 5. Remove the ones digit. What do you notice? Why did this happen?

Celebrating Fraction Birthdays

Relating division to fractions

Daniel sent this invitation.

My sister Katie is 6 months old. Please come to her half-birthday party on Sunday afternoon at 3 o'clock. And bring half a present.

Daniel

P.S. You have to tell a whole story about the half present.

from *The Half-Birthday Party*
by Charlotte Pomerantz

What is half of this present?

All of these show that half of 20 rings is 10.

$\frac{1}{2}$ of 20 = 10   20 ÷ 2 = 10   2)‾20‾ = 10

Which way would you write it? Why?

Work in a group.

Model using fraction mats and counters. Write a sentence with a fraction and a division sentence when appropriate.

1. What is one half of each present? What is one fourth? one third?

2. A half present is 50 blocks. What would be the whole present? What if 50 blocks are a one-fourth present?

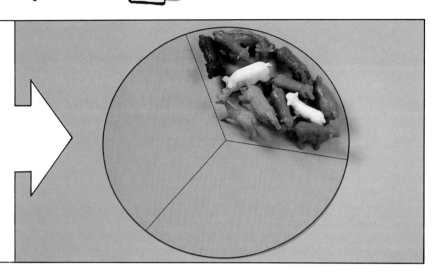

3. Twelve farm animals are a present for a one-third birthday. What would be the present for a two-thirds birthday?

4. Eight picture books are a present for a one-year birthday. What would be the present for a $1\frac{1}{2}$ year birthday?

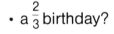

5. Four shapes are a present for a one-third birthday. What would be the present for

- a $\frac{2}{3}$ birthday?
- a $\frac{3}{3}$ birthday?
- a $\frac{4}{3}$ birthday?

6. A present for a one-half birthday is 100 building pieces and a one-year birthday is 200 building pieces. What would be the present for a three-fourths birthday?

7. What is about half of this present?

8. Which would you choose to make a present for a two-thirds birthday? Explain.

9. What present would you bring to a fraction birthday party? Write a story about it. Tell how you determined how much to bring.

Your femur or thigh bone makes up about one quarter of your height.
Estimate its length.

Sharing Food

The Aesop fable "Lion's Share" tells the story of a lion, tiger, leopard, and jackal sharing food.

"The first piece," said the Lion, "is for me because I am the Lion. The second piece is for the bravest, and that's me again. The third piece is for the strongest, and there's no doubt that I am stronger than any of you. As for the fourth piece—I dare anyone to touch it!"

from *Aesop's Fables* selected and adapted by Louis Untermeyer

What fraction would each animal get if they shared the food equally?

How many pieces would each of the 4 animals get if they shared 85 pieces equally?

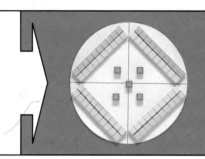

Why can the remainder be written as a fraction?

$$85 \div 4 = 21 + R1$$
$$85 \div 4 = 21\frac{1}{4}$$

Work in a group.

Use fraction mats and base ten blocks.

1. How many pieces would each get if 75 pieces are shared equally among 4? 2? 6?
   Write each remainder as a fraction.

2. Choose a 2-digit number greater than 30 to represent a number of pieces to be shared equally.
   Predict the fraction remainder when shared among 2   3   5   10.

   Then check your predictions by dividing.

3. The lion takes half of 100 pieces. The 3 other animals share equally what is left. How many pieces does each get?

4. Each of 3 animals receives $5\frac{2}{3}$ pieces. How many pieces are shared?

5. What lesson was Aesop trying to tell? What do you think "a lion's share" means?

94

TAKE YOUR PICK

GREATEST NUMBER

The quotient is 2 greater than the remainder when you divide a number by 6.
What is the greatest number you could be dividing?

MISSING SYMBOLS

Place the symbols +, ×, and = to make a true sentence.

1   8   4   4   2

Then place the symbols ÷, =, and + R to make another true sentence. Tell what you notice.

COMPARING AGES

Wayne is one half as old as Lena.
Lena is one third as old as Mom.
Mom is over 30 years old.
How old might each person be?
What if Mom is 33 years old?

FITTING RECTANGLES

What is the greatest number of 2 by 3 rectangles you can fit on a 9 by 10 rectangle without overlapping or cutting?

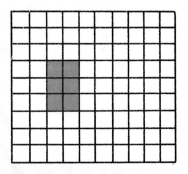

CALCULATOR FRACTIONS

How can a calculator be used to find

$\frac{1}{3}$ of 435?

$\frac{2}{3}$ of 435?

$\frac{7}{8}$ of 1000?

Make up other problems. Post them on the bulletin board for your classmates to solve.

Joan drove 80 km in 1 h. For the first 30 min, she drove at a speed of 60 km/h. What was her speed for the rest of the hour?

Placing Racing Flags

Five flags are equally spaced around the perimeter of a 200 cm race track.
How far apart are the flags?

Lise is using the fact that $20 \div 5 = 4$.

$$5 \overline{)200} \rightarrow 5 \overline{)20 \text{ tens}} \quad \overset{4 \text{ tens or } 40}{}$$

Use a different way to find how far apart the flags are.
How would the answer change if the track was 400 cm long?

Work in a group.

Use facts you know.

1. Find the distance between each pair of flags.
   Write each division sentence.

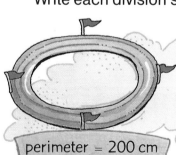

perimeter = 200 cm   perimeter = 300 cm   perimeter = 540 cm

2. Make up and solve a racing flag problem for each division.

$800 \div 2$ $3 \overline{)900}$ $1200 \div 4$

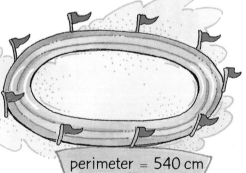

96

3. Show how the fact 45 ÷ 5 = 9 can help you find the distance between each pair of flags.

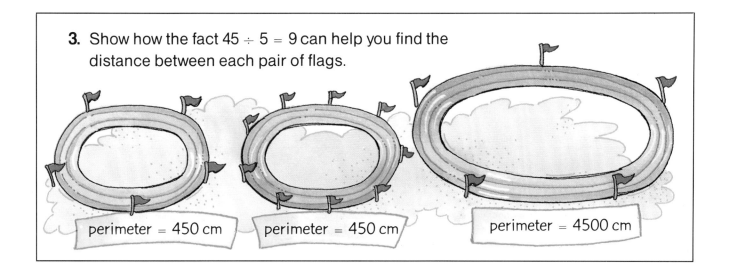

perimeter = 450 cm   perimeter = 450 cm   perimeter = 4500 cm

4. Copy and complete the table. What patterns do you notice?

Perimeter in centimetres	30	300	3000
Number of flags	5	5	5
Distance between flags	?	?	?

5. Use digits that will make a true statement. Make up a racing flag problem for it.

$$\boxed{?}\,00$$
$$\boxed{?}\,)\,\overline{\boxed{?}\,\boxed{?}\,00}$$

6. Find the distance between the flags on the first two tracks. Then show how those answers can be used to find the distance between the flags on the last track.

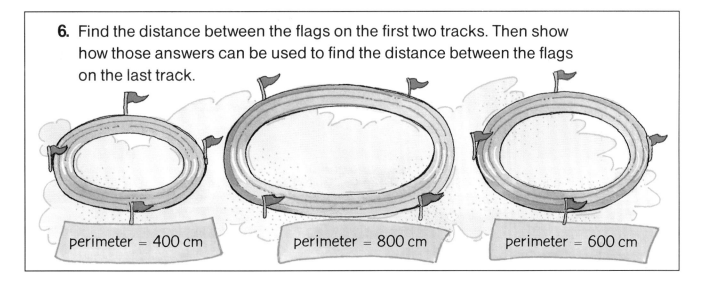

perimeter = 400 cm   perimeter = 800 cm   perimeter = 600 cm

7. How many centimetres are between each pair of flags on these race tracks?

- 6 flags equally spaced around a 3 m track
- 12 flags equally spaced around a 6 m track

8. Which division is easiest for you to do? Explain. Make up a racing flag problem for it.

$$7\,)\,\overline{96} \qquad 3\,)\,\overline{600} \qquad 2\,)\,\overline{479}$$

Each day Karen painted twice as much of a long fence as she did the day before. It took her 30 days to paint the entire fence. After how many days was the fence half painted?

Small animal groups have special names.

a band of gorillas
a brood of chicks
a cloud of gnats
a clowder of cats
a colony of ants
a crash of rhinoceroses
a cry of hounds
a drift of swine
a flock of birds

a gaggle of geese
a gang of elks
a knot of toads
a mob of kangaroos
a murder of crows
a pod of whales
a sloth of bears
a troop of monkeys
a yoke of oxen

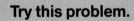

Try this problem.

A mob of 271 kangaroos split up into 4 almost equal groups. Each group hopped in a different direction. About how many kangaroos hopped in each direction?

Linda used a different division fact.

Ravi used a division fact he knew.

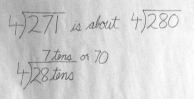

$4\overline{)271}$ is about $4\overline{)280}$

$\dfrac{7 \text{ tens} \text{ or } 70}{4\overline{)28 \text{ tens}}}$

$4\overline{)271}$ is about $4\overline{)240}$

$\dfrac{6 \text{ tens} \text{ or } 60}{4\overline{)24 \text{ tens}}}$

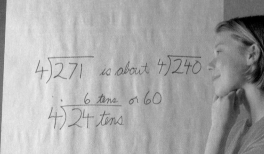

How could you use both estimates to find a better estimate?

98

Work in a group.

Use facts you know to help you estimate.
Explain how you estimated.

1. About half of a knot of 191 toads sat on a log. About how many toads were not sitting on the log?

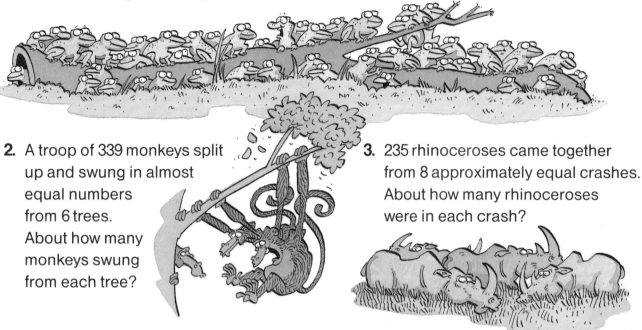

2. A troop of 339 monkeys split up and swung in almost equal numbers from 6 trees. About how many monkeys swung from each tree?

3. 235 rhinoceroses came together from 8 approximately equal crashes. About how many rhinoceroses were in each crash?

Explain how each pair of calculations can help you solve the problem.
Then make up another problem that each pair could help you solve.

4. A colony of 3782 ants built 5 nests. About how many ants can live in each nest?

$$\begin{array}{r} 700 \\ 5\overline{)3500} \end{array} \qquad \begin{array}{r} 800 \\ 5\overline{)4000} \end{array}$$

5. A gaggle of geese migrated 3000 km in 1 week. About how far did they travel each day?

$$\begin{array}{r} 400 \\ \times\ 7 \\ \hline 2800 \end{array} \qquad \begin{array}{r} 500 \\ \times\ 7 \\ \hline 3500 \end{array}$$

Use a fact you know to estimate. How can you get a closer estimate?

6. A murder of crows flew to 463 farms in 6 weeks. About how many farms did they fly to each week?

Make up division estimating problems for another group to solve.

7. Use any animal group name listed.

8. Use an animal group name that is not listed.

Draw the shape of the cross section when a cheese tube is cut like this.

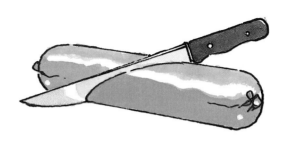

Delivering Flyers

Four friends agreed to share the delivery of 135 flyers as equally as possible.

How many flyers should each deliver?

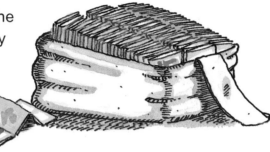

Angela renamed the dividend.

Leon renamed the dividend differently.

$$\begin{array}{r} 30 + 3 + R3 \\ 4\overline{)135} \to 4\overline{)120 + 12 + 3} \end{array}$$

$$\begin{array}{r} 20 + 10 + 3 + R3 \\ 4\overline{)135} \to 4\overline{)80 + 40 + 12 + 3} \end{array}$$

Why did she choose these numbers? Finish her work.

Explain why he chose these numbers. Finish his work.

Show another way to divide 135 by 4 by renaming the dividend.

Work in a group.

Rename the dividends with numbers you can divide easily by the divisors.

1. Show how each number of friends can deliver 205 flyers as equally as possible.

   3   5   9

WELCOME

2. Rename 260 flyers two different ways to show how they can be delivered equally by 5 friends.

3. Which renaming would you use to divide 345 flyers by 4? Explain.

$$4 \overline{)\ 300 + 40 + 4 + 1}$$

$$4 \overline{)\ 200 + 100 + 44 + 1}$$

$$4 \overline{)\ 320 + 24 + 1}$$

4. Rename the number of flyers to help you divide each by 6. Which did you find easiest to divide? Explain.

612   558   1212   672

5. Use any digit so that the flyers can be divided equally.

$\boxed{?}$ 02 flyers delivered by 2

832 flyers delivered by $\boxed{?}$

54 $\boxed{?}$ flyers delivered by 5

6. Find a 3-digit number of flyers that can be divided equally among 2, 3, or 4 friends. What is the least 3-digit number that works? the greatest?

7. Five friends are delivering 800 flyers altogether. They are being paid 4¢ for each flyer. How much money should each receive? How long would it take the friends to deliver the flyers?

How many times would you have to write your first name to have more than 1000 letters?

Sharing the Booty

Each of 6 salvage hunters receives an equal share of 96 boots.

What division does this suggest?

Philip found each boat's share.

Then he found each individual's share.

Explain why this method divides the boots into 6 equal shares.

Work in a group.

Use only halves, thirds, and fifths mats.

1. Find the share of each item for 6 salvage hunters.

   72 tires   132 bottles
   150 fishing lures

2. Show how 120 boots can be shared equally among each number of salvage hunters.

   4   8   6   10   12

3. Which number of shares cannot be found using the fraction mats you have? Explain.

   7   8   9   10   11

4. Share 1000 bottles among 10 salvage hunters.
   For what other number of salvage hunters could you use the same two mats to find equal shares of 1000 bottles?

102

Take Your pick

CALCULATOR PATTERN

Complete each division.
What patterns do you notice?
What might be the next division?
Make up a similar pattern
starting with a different division.

62 ÷ 5

124 ÷ 10

248 ÷ 20

SOUTHPAWS

There is about 1 left-handed
person for every 10 right-handed
people.
Estimate the number of
left-handed people in

- your class 30
- your school 300
- your community 300,000

SHARING PHONE LISTS

A list of numbers to be phoned was divided equally between 2 students.
Each of those students divided their lists equally among 3 other students.
Each of those students divided their lists equally among 5 other students.
What might have been the number of phone numbers on the list?

OOPS! 466

Keith was dividing 456 by 5 on his
calculator but pressed the wrong
button. He divided 466 instead.
How can he correct his mistake
without starting over?

PICKING DIGITS

How many pairs of digits can
you use so that the answer is a
whole number?

6 ? ÷ ?

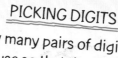

**Make up other problems. Post them
on the bulletin board for your
classmates to solve.**

Draw a pentagon. Connect the vertices not already connected by sides. Do you think this action always creates a star in a pentagon? What shape is in the centre of the star?

Comparing Prices

Often we compare prices by finding the price of one part. This is called the **unit price.**

Anya is dividing 175 by 2 to find the price in cents of one box from the first ad.

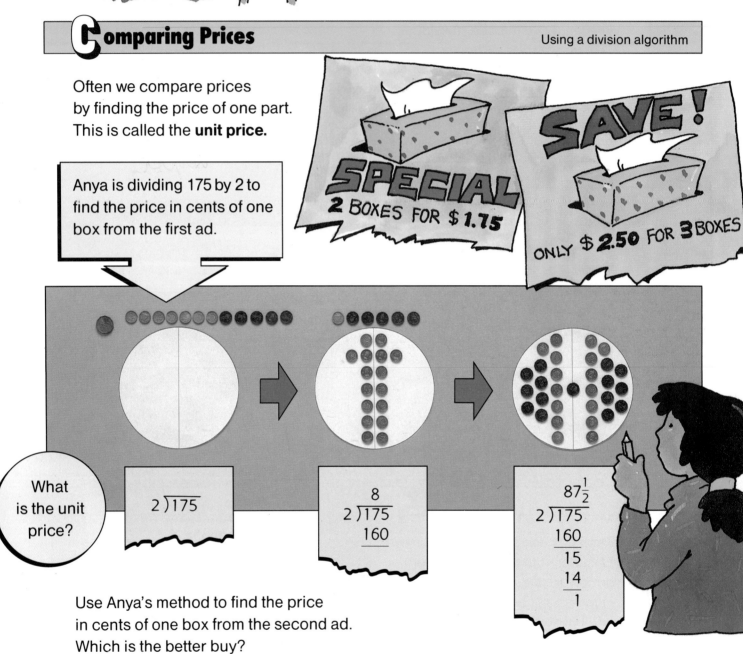

SPECIAL 2 BOXES FOR $1.75

SAVE! ONLY $2.50 FOR 3 BOXES

What is the unit price?

$$2\overline{)175}$$

$$\begin{array}{r} 8 \\ 2\overline{)175} \\ 160 \end{array}$$

$$\begin{array}{r} 87\frac{1}{2} \\ 2\overline{)175} \\ 160 \\ \hline 15 \\ 14 \\ \hline 1 \end{array}$$

Use Anya's method to find the price in cents of one box from the second ad. Which is the better buy?

Work in a group.

Use play money and fraction mats.

1. Find the better buy. Explain your method.

2 for $1.89

5 for $4.65

104

2. What is the price of one muffin? What would you expect to pay for 10 muffins?

8 for $4.72

3. Find the better buy using two different methods.

$2.97

AA BATTERIES

$5.75

AA BATTERIES

4. How many plants would you expect to be able to buy for $10.50?

SPECIAL
3 for $5.25

5. What would you expect to pay for 4 binders?

3
for
$8.79

6. Write a price between $1.00 and $10.00 and a number of items from 2 to 9 on a slip of paper. Give the paper to another group member to find the unit price. Then order all the unit prices from least to greatest.

$7.50
for
8

7. Use flyers, catalogues, and ads. Find at least 3 items sold in quantity. Find their unit prices. Then estimate what you would expect to pay for several more of each.

8. Do any stores where your family shops display unit prices? What type of stores are they? Why do you think they do this?

9. When might the lowest unit price not be the best buy?

```
  111
  333
  555
  777
+ 999
```

Rewrite this addition leaving out as many digits as necessary so that the sum is 1111.

F inding Prizes

Every 7th bottle cap shows a prize.
How many prizes are there in a shipment of 950 caps?

Lia is dividing 950 by 7 to find the number of prizes.

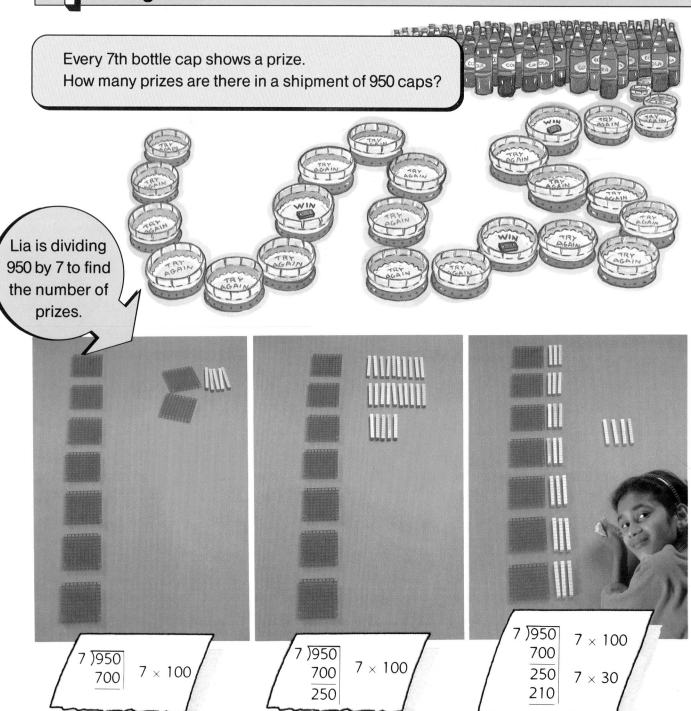

```
    ___
  7)950      7 × 100
    700
```

```
    ___
  7)950      7 × 100
    700
    ___
    250
```

```
    ___
  7)950      7 × 100
    700
    ___
    250      7 × 30
    210
```

Finish her work. Check your answer by dividing another way.

106

Work in a group.

Use base ten blocks. Check your answers by dividing another way or by multiplying.

1. How many prizes are there in a shipment of 264 bottles if a prize is shown under every second cap? third cap? fourth cap?

2. One cap in each carton shows a prize. How many prizes are there in a shipment of 750 bottles?

3. Prizes are under every fifth cap. Show how the multiplication fact $120 \times 5 = 600$ can help you find the number of prizes in

   615 caps   585 caps

4. Prizes are shown under every eighth cap. How many prizes are there in a shipment of 8920 bottles?

5. Every third cap shows a prize. Every eighth prize is double the value of the others.
   How many prizes are there in a shipment of 975 bottles?
   How many prizes are double the value of the others?

6. Use your answer for Problem 5 to help you answer this one. Every 24th cap shows this.

   How many caps show NEXT BOTTLE FREE in a shipment of 975 bottles?

7. Now try this one. Every 15th cap shows a prize. How many prizes are there in a shipment of 990 bottles?

8. Make up a division problem about prizes for another group to solve.

There are lots of ways to calculate 268 ÷ 4.
Here are some. Can you think of any more?

1. You might rename 268 as a sum of numbers easily divided by 4.

$$\begin{array}{r} 60 + 7 = 67 \\ \hline 4 \overline{)\ 240 + 28} \end{array}$$

268 ÷ 4 = 67

2. You could rename 268 as a difference of numbers easily divided by 4.

$$\begin{array}{r} 70 - 3 = 67 \\ \hline 4 \overline{)\ 280 - 12} \end{array}$$

268 ÷ 4 = 67

3. You might divide 268 in half twice.

$\frac{1}{2}$ of 268 $\frac{1}{2}$ of 134

268 ÷ 2 = 134   134 ÷ 2 = 67

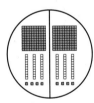   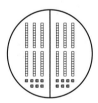

268 ÷ 4 = 67

4. You could multiply and subtract in steps.

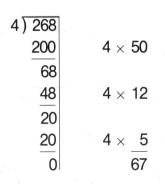

$$\begin{array}{r} 4 \overline{)\ 268} \\ 200 \\ \hline 68 \\ 48 \\ \hline 20 \\ 20 \\ \hline 0 \end{array}$$
4 × 50
4 × 12
4 × 5
—
67

268 ÷ 4 = 67

Work in a group.

Show 2 different ways
to do each division.

1. 137 ÷ 3   **2.** 4) 96

3. 6) 288   **4.** 1000 ÷ 4

5. 5) 275   **6.** 8) 699

Take Your Pick

DECIMAL REMAINDERS

Choose 5 odd numbers.
Use a calculator to divide each number by 2.
What do you notice about each answer?
Now divide each of your odd numbers by 4.
What do you notice now?

PLACING DIGITS

Place the digits 1, 3, 5, 7, and 9 to make the
- greatest quotient
- least quotient

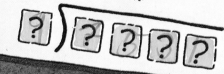

COUNTING SIT-UPS

Louis Scorpio Jr. set a world record when he did 60 405 sit-ups in 24 h. To achieve his record, about how many did he have to do each hour? each minute?

ANCIENT CAPACITY MEASURES

Many centuries ago, people used the following units to measure amounts of liquids.

2 mouthfuls = 1 jigger
2 jiggers = 1 jack
2 jacks = 1 jill
2 jills = 1 cup

How many cups are needed to hold 256 mouthfuls?

Make up a similar problem for someone else to solve.

FEDERAL ELECTIONS

The federal government must hold an election at least every 5 years. At least how many elections have been held since Canada was formed in 1867?
Explain why Canada had only 18 prime ministers by its 125th birthday in 1992.

Make up other problems. Post them on the bulletin board for your classmates to solve.

Try this problem before going on.

MARBLES

Jerry has half as many marbles as Billy. Billy has one third as many as Harry. Harry has one quarter as many as Garry. How many marbles does each boy have if Garry has 240 marbles?

Cecilia's group solved the problem by working backwards.

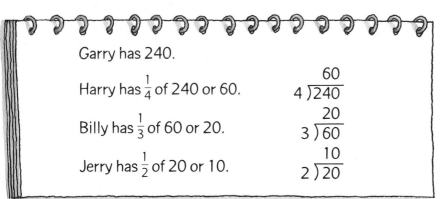

Garry has 240.

Harry has $\frac{1}{4}$ of 240 or 60.

$$4\overline{)240} \quad \frac{60}{}$$

Billy has $\frac{1}{3}$ of 60 or 20.

$$3\overline{)60} \quad \frac{20}{}$$

Jerry has $\frac{1}{2}$ of 20 or 10.

$$2\overline{)20} \quad \frac{10}{}$$

What if Garry had only 72 marbles?

Work with a partner.

Solve each problem by working backwards.

SHARING JELLY BEANS

Sally shared her jelly beans with Kelly and Millie. Each girl received an equal number with one left over. Then Kelly shared her jelly beans with Jenny. Each girl received an equal number with one left over. How many jelly beans did Sally start with if Jenny received 12?

WANDERING ANT

An ant walked 5 cm across this page, turned and walked down 6 cm, turned and walked across 5 cm. It ended up at the bottom left corner. Where could it have started?

EATING APPLES

An elephant ate half a basket of apples on Sunday. Then it ate half the remaining apples on Monday. Each day it ate half the remaining apples until on Saturday there was only one apple left to eat. How many apples were in the basket on Sunday?

110

Practising What You've Learned

Write a problem for each of these. Then solve.

1. 48 ÷ 3

2. $\frac{1}{8}$ of 96

3. 5) 1000

4.

Solve ONLY the problems where you could use division.

5. About how many days are there in one quarter of a year?

6. A restaurant uses 4 dozen eggs each day. How many eggs does it use in a week? in a month?

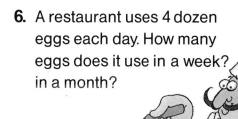

7. The sides of a hexagon are equal in length. The perimeter is 90 cm. What is the length of each side?

8. A 49 cm long piece of ribbon is cut exactly in half. How long is each piece?

9. Joanne bought 5 cassette tapes costing $2.98 each. How much change will she receive from a $20 bill?

10. Edward trades 128 pennies for nickels. How many nickels does he receive? How many more pennies does he need to receive another nickel?

11. Which is the better buy for the same type of socks?

5 pairs for $8.95
2 pairs for $3.65

12. Jay's family drove 645 km in 3 days. About how far did they drive each day?

111

Playing Games for Practice

Play each game in a group of 2, 3, or 4.

Divide and Conquer

- Remove the face cards and aces from a deck of playing cards.
- Shuffle the cards and place them face down in a pile.
- Turn over the top card.
- Place a counter on any unoccupied number on a 100 chart that can be divided evenly by the number on your card.
- Each player uses a different color of counters.
- Take turns until no unoccupied numbers can be divided evenly by the numbers on the cards.
- The player with the greatest number of counters on the chart is the winner.

Variation: The player having the greatest sum of the numbers under the counters is the winner.

Example

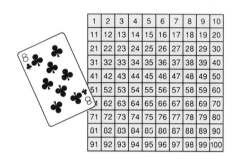

A counter could be placed on 32.
What other numbers are possible?

Rolling Fraction Remainders

- Roll one die twice to get a 2-digit dividend using the digits in the order rolled.
- Roll the die again to get a 1-digit divisor.
- Divide and find the fraction remainder.
- Place a counter on any unoccupied space showing a fraction equal to your remainder.
- Each player uses a different color of counters.
- Take turns until the board is covered with counters.
- The winner is the player with the greatest number of counters on the board.

Example

$$15\tfrac{1}{3}$$
$$3\overline{)46}$$
$$\underline{30}$$
$$16$$
$$\underline{15}$$
$$1$$

Place a counter on $\tfrac{1}{3}$ or $\tfrac{2}{6}$.

$\frac{0}{2}$	$\frac{1}{2}$	$\frac{0}{3}$	$\frac{1}{3}$	$\frac{2}{3}$
$\frac{0}{4}$	$\frac{1}{4}$	$\frac{2}{4}$	$\frac{3}{4}$	$\frac{0}{5}$
$\frac{1}{5}$	$\frac{2}{5}$	$\frac{3}{5}$	$\frac{4}{5}$	$\frac{0}{6}$
$\frac{1}{6}$	$\frac{2}{6}$	$\frac{3}{6}$	$\frac{4}{6}$	$\frac{5}{6}$

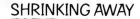

SHRINKING AWAY

Suppose you find that each day you are half as tall as you were the day before. In how many days will you be shorter than your pencil? On what day will you be able to walk under the classroom door?

LEFTOVER DOLLARS

You get to keep any leftover $1 coins after sharing 100 of them equally among less than 9 young children. Among how many children would you prefer to share them? Why?

BLAST FROM THE PAST

Solve this problem given to students in 1869.

A school has 3 classrooms.
$\frac{1}{4}$ of the boys are in the first classroom.
$\frac{1}{4}$ of the boys are in the second.
20 boys are in the third.

How many boys are in each classroom?

LEAP YEARS

How many days are in a leap year? Any year that can be divided evenly by 4 is a leap year, except century years, which must be divided evenly by 400.
Is this year a leap year?
Is 2000 a leap year?
What leap years will occur before you are 50?

DIVIDING BY 7

Use a calculator to divide each number from 7 to 13 by 7. Record each decimal remainder. Describe any patterns you see. Predict the decimal remainders when numbers from 14 to 20 are divided by 7. Check your prediction by dividing.

Make up other problems. Post them on the bulletin board for your classmates to solve.

1. Make up and solve a division problem for each situation.

2. Use two different non-zero digits that will allow you to divide in your head.

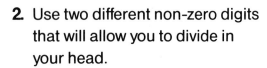

3. How does knowing $420 \div 6$ help you find $432 \div 6$?

4. Show how to use this fraction mat to share these crayons among 8 students.

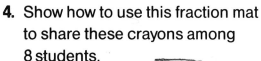
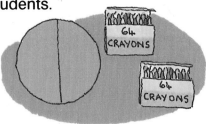

5. Use any number.

$\boxed{?} \times 2 \times 2 \times 2 \div 8 =$

Try other numbers. What happens? Explain why.

6. If you cut and tape squares of paper, how many nets of cubes can you make from a 10×10 grid?

7. Six friends shared a bag of apples. Each received $2\frac{1}{3}$ apples. How many apples were in the bag originally?

8. Without doing the actual calculations, decide which answer is closest to 500. Explain what you did.

$4 \overline{)3487}$ $5 \overline{)2598}$ $8 \overline{)4862}$

9. What digits make this sentence true?

$\frac{1}{\boxed{?}}$ of $240 > 59$

10. A 3-digit number is divided by 8 using a calculator. Which is a reasonable answer?

5.825   58.25   582.5

Thinking Back

How would you explain to a friend how to correct this error?

$$6\overline{)1212} = 22$$

How could you still solve sharing problems if division was banned?

Explain how division might be used to find how many pickets are needed for a fence.

How many cars are needed to take 18 students to the museum if 4 students travel in each car? Which answer makes the most sense? Tell why.

4        $4\frac{1}{2}$ 5

Which division would you rather do in your head? Why?

$$4\overline{)2000} \qquad 7\overline{)169}$$

What questions do you still have about division?

Examining

▼ Which would you more likely measure the mass of in grams? in kilograms?

Name two other things you would measure in each unit.

Which unit would you want to use to measure the distance from your home to your school? Why? ▶

centimetre   metre   kilometre

▼ What might the 10 cm describe?

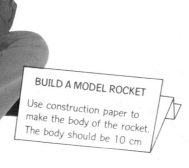

▼ What containers have capacities between 5 L and 10 L?

BUILD A MODEL ROCKET

Use construction paper to make the body of the rocket. The body should be 10 cm

Measurement

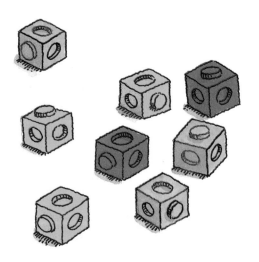

How many different prisms can you build with 7 cubes? 8 cubes? Tell what you notice.

For each colored square, what is the perimeter? the area?

Use grid paper. Draw a square where the number describing its perimeter is

- equal to the number describing its area
- greater than the number describing its area
- less than the number describing its area

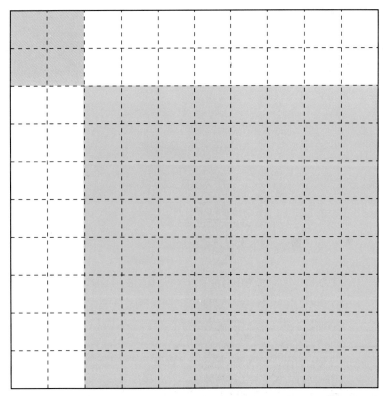

Which measurement— mass, volume, length, or width— is most useful to describe a pencil? Tell why.

Describe and continue this pattern.
3 × 4
33 × 34
333 × 334

 Mapping Out a Trip

Estimating and measuring distances

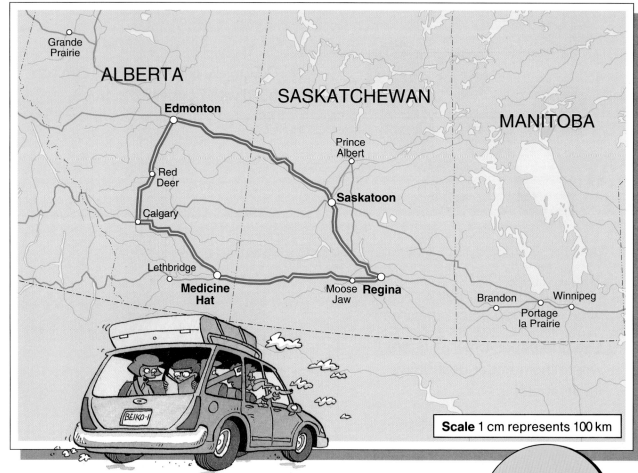

Scale 1 cm represents 100 km

The Beiko family lives in Regina. They took a car trip to visit relatives in Medicine Hat, Edmonton, and Saskatoon. Then they returned home.

What does 1 cm on the map represent?

Why do you need to know the scale of the map to estimate the total distance they travelled?

1. Estimate the trip distance using
   • a ruler   • a string
   How close are your estimates?
   Which estimation method is better? Why?

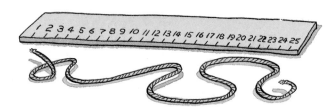

2. A distance chart shows the distance between cities.
   Why are some boxes empty on the chart?

Distance	Edmonton	Medicine Hat	Regina	Saskatoon
Edmonton		524 km	843 km	526 km
Medicine Hat	524 km		515 km	462 km
Regina	843 km	515 km		254 km
Saskatoon	526 km	462 km	254 km	

Use the chart to estimate the distance the Beiko family travelled.
How does this compare with your estimates from Problem 1?

3. A driving time chart shows the time it takes to drive between cities at an
   average speed of 80 km/h.

Time	Edmonton	Medicine Hat	Regina	Saskatoon
Edmonton		6.5 h	10.5 h	6.6 h
Medicine Hat	6.5 h		6.4 h	5.8 h
Regina	10.5 h	6.4 h		3.2 h
Saskatoon	6.6 h	5.8 h	3.2h	

What distance is driven in 1 h? 2 h? 3 h? 0.1 h?
Use the chart to estimate the distance the Beiko family travelled.
Is this distance the same as the distance you found using the
distance chart? Explain.

4. Map out another round trip. Go through at
   least 3 cities for a total distance that is

   • less than the Beiko family travelled
   • more than the Beiko family travelled

   Create a distance chart or a driving time
   chart for the cities in one of your trips.

5. Why do some road maps include distance
   charts and others, driving time charts?
   Do they both give the same information?
   Which do you think is more useful in planning a trip? Explain.

What are three other numbers that might be in the first group and not in the second group? Why?

| 132 | 374 | | 133 | 371 |
| 242 | 583 | | 245 | 580 |

Examining Animal Tracks

What are you measuring when you find the amount of surface something covers?

How would you estimate the area of the skunk's hind foot track?

Clark traced it onto centimetre grid paper.
Then he counted the squares where the track covered half or more.
He didn't count squares where the track covered less than half.

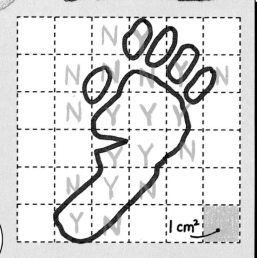

1 cm²

1. What is the approximate area in square centimetres (cm²) using this method?

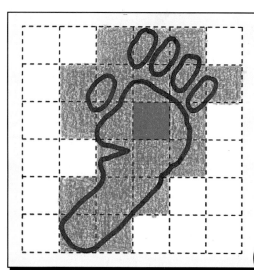

Arnie also traced it onto grid paper.
He counted the squares that contained any part of the track.
Then he counted the squares that were completely within the track.
Then he found their average.

2. What is the approximate area using this method?

120

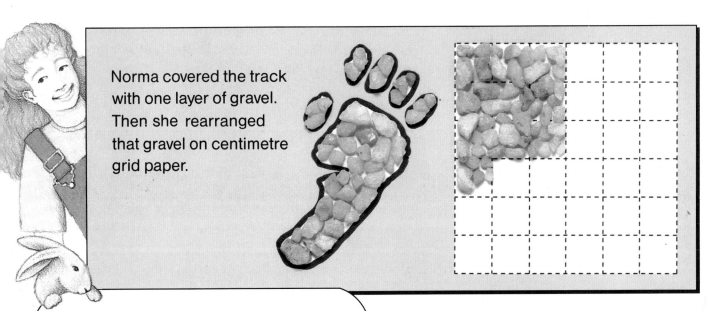

Norma covered the track with one layer of gravel. Then she rearranged that gravel on centimetre grid paper.

3. What is the approximate area using this method?

4. Which method do you prefer? Why? Can you think of any other methods?

Work in a group.

Use centimetre grid paper.

5. Estimate the area of each track using two methods. Which track do you think belongs to each animal?

cat   dog   cottontail rabbit   muskrat   beaver

What does $\frac{1}{4}$ size mean? Why is it used?

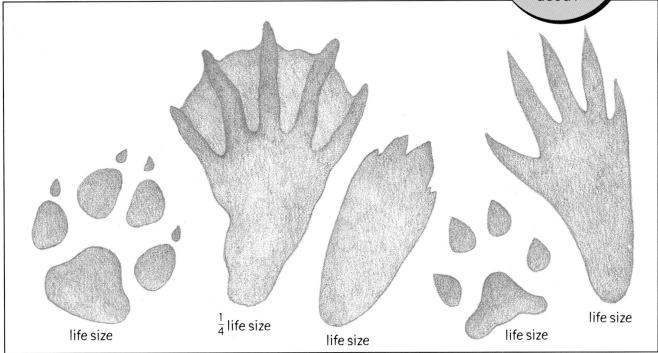

life size $\frac{1}{4}$ life size   life size   life size   life size

6. What are some of the features that make the animal tracks different? Which of those differences are mathematical?

Multiply 38 and 99 in your head.
Explain to a classmate how you did it.

Modelling Sports Surfaces

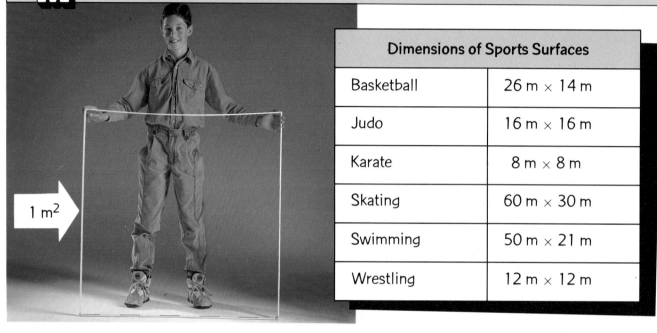

1 m²

Dimensions of Sports Surfaces	
Basketball	26 m × 14 m
Judo	16 m × 16 m
Karate	8 m × 8 m
Skating	60 m × 30 m
Swimming	50 m × 21 m
Wrestling	12 m × 12 m

Sonja made a model of one of the sports surfaces on grid paper.

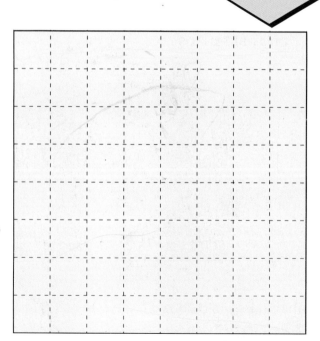

Which sports surface did she model?

1. What is the area of the model in square centimetres (cm²)?
   What is the actual area in square metres (m²)?
   What is the perimeter of the model?
   What is the actual perimeter?

1 cm represents 1 m

1 cm² represents 1 m²

122

Work in a group.

Use centimetre grid paper.

2. Model the other sports surfaces.

3. Order the surfaces from greatest to least area. Tell how you decided the order.

4. Order the surfaces from greatest to least perimeter. Tell how you decided the order.

5. Cut out your model of the judo surface. Cut and rearrange it into a rectangle in two different ways.
   Do your rectangles and the square have the same area? the same perimeter? Explain.
   Why do you think the judo surface is square?

6. Cut a string the length of the perimeter for each of two other surfaces. Rearrange each string to make the area of

   • one greater than its original
   • the other less than its original

   Compare these shapes with the original surface.

7. If you know a surface has a perimeter of 60 m, would you know what shape it must be? Explain.

8. Does knowing the area of a surface tell you its shape? Explain.

9. Why do sports have playing surfaces with different areas?
   Which sport do you think has the playing surface with the greatest area?

CUTTING CORNERS

Cut 2 cm² from one corner of a 4 cm by 4 cm square.

Cut 3 cm² from the next corner.
Cut 2 cm² from the next corner.
What is the greatest perimeter possible for the remaining shape?
What is the least perimeter?

VACATION TRIP

Pick a place you would like to spend a vacation that you could drive to from where you live. Use maps to estimate the distance to get there.

PAIRS OF RECTANGLES

By how much do the areas of these rectangles differ?
By how do the perimeters differ?

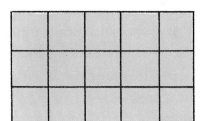

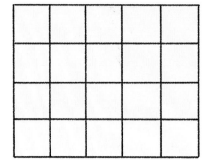

Draw another rectangle so that it and the green rectangle have areas differing by 10 cm² and perimeters differing by 4 cm.
Then draw another rectangle so that it and the yellow rectangle have areas differing by 4 cm² and perimeters differing by 2 cm.

GIVE ME A HAND

Estimate the area of one side of your hand. Then estimate the amount of fabric needed to make a mitten for your hand.

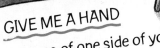

30 PLEASE

Use a loop of string. Make as many different shapes as you can with a perimeter of 30 cm. Which appears to have the greatest area? the least?

Make up the other problems. Post them on the bulletin board for your classmates to solve.

List the first ten multiples of 8.
Add the digits of each multiple until a single digit results.
Describe the pattern.
Repeat this with the first ten multiples of 7.

Measuring the Volume of Food Boxes

Using cubic centimetres

Why do you think we say the volume of a unit cube is 1 cm^3 (cubic centimetre)?

What are you measuring when you find volume?

What is the volume of a

 rod?   a flat?   a large cube?

1. What is the volume of this box?

Work with a partner.

Use base ten blocks to model food boxes.

2. Estimate and then find the volume of some of your food boxes.
List them from least to greatest volume.

3. Are most of the volumes less than or more than 100 cm^3?

4. Estimate the volume of a large cereal box.
Which blocks would you use to help you find the volume?

5. Do you think that the volume of this box is the same as the volume of its contents? Tell how you would find out.

125

About $\frac{1}{3}$ of our body mass is in our legs.

Estimate the mass of one of your legs in kilograms.

Here is the net of a box that is open on top.

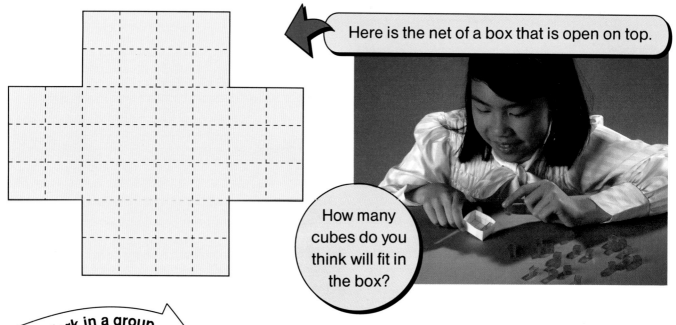

How many cubes do you think will fit in the box?

Use centimetre grid paper and centimetre cubes.

1. Build an open box from each of these nets and the net above. Fill each with cubes.

What is the volume of each box in cubic centimetres?
How do the volumes compare? Explain.

2. Predict the volume of this open box.
   Test your prediction.
   How could you find the volume without
   actually filling the box?

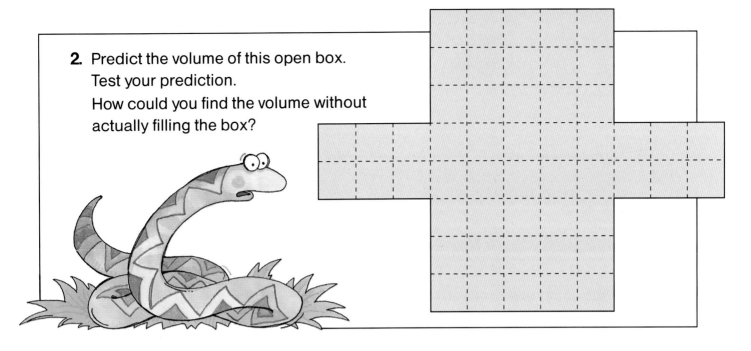

3. How can you use the net to predict
   this box's height? length? width?

4. Build nets for open boxes with
   volumes of 13 cm^3 and 17 cm^3.
   How many nets are possible for each
   box?
   How are the nets alike?

5. Can you make a net for an open box
   with a volume of 21 cm^3 that is
   4 cm high? Explain.

6. Make a net for an open box that is twice
   as long, twice as wide, and twice as
   high as this one.
   How do the volumes of the two boxes
   compare?

7. Brent said that counting the squares
   in the net tells you the volume of its
   box. Do you agree?
   Explain.

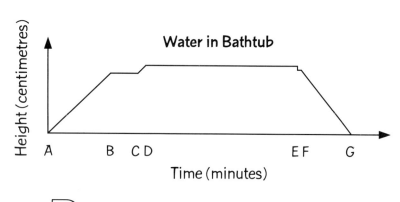

Water in Bathtub

Height (centimetres)

Time (minutes)

A   B   C D   E F   G

What might be happening at times A, B, C, D, E, F, and G?

Packing a Truck to Move

Using cubic metres

The Almeida family is packing to move.

1 m   1 m³   1 m   1 m

Why do you think we say that this box has a volume of one cubic metre?
What household items take up about 1 m³ of space?

1. This mattress set is to be moved. How many cubic metres of space does it take up? Explain.

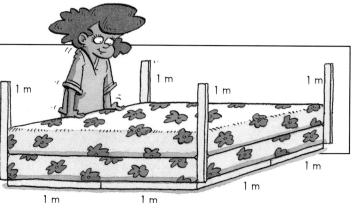

1 m   1 m   1 m   1 m   1 m   1 m   1 m   1 m

2. Another mattress set is a bit less than 1 m³.
   Describe or draw what it might look like.

Work in a group.

3. About how much space does this sofa take up? Explain.

1 m   1 m   1 m

128

4. Estimate the number of cubic metres needed to move this living room furniture. Explain your thinking.

5. The Almeida's have about 1000 books. About how many cubic metres of space might the books take up? Tell how you decided.

6. They are renting a truck to move their 33 m³ of belongings.
Estimate the volume of each rental truck in the chart.
Which of the trucks are large enough for their belongings?

	Truck	Dimensions			Rental Charge	
		length	width	height	each day	each kilometre
Rent a Truck	A	2.9 m	1.7 m	1.4 m	$32.95	18 ¢
	B	4.6 m	2.3 m	2.0 m	$39.95	18 ¢
	C	7.3 m	2.4 m	2.2 m	$59.95	22 ¢
You Move It	D	3.5 m	2.3 m	2.1 m	$29.95	35 ¢
	E	4.3 m	2.3 m	2.2 m	$34.95	35 ¢
	F	6.8 m	2.3 m	2.6 m	$44.95	39 ¢

2.9 is about 3
1.7 is about 2
1.4 is about 1
6 cubes so 6 m³

Does the longest truck always have the greatest volume? Explain.

7. Which truck that will hold their belongings has the lower cost if they
- are moving locally?
- are moving about 400 km away?

Tell five things about this shape.

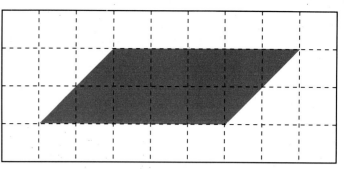

Comparing Dinosaur Masses

Would the kilogram be a good unit to measure the mass of a real dinosaur? Explain.

Would the gram be a better unit? Explain.

If you created a unit to measure the mass of a dinosaur, what would you call it? Why?

Sometimes, we use the **tonne** as a unit of mass.

How many kilograms is 1 t (tonne)?

Work with a partner. **Use the chart.**

1. Express the mass of each dinosaur in kilograms.

Dinosaur	Mass
Brachiosaurus	77 t
Diplodocus	10.6 t
Stegosaurus	1.8 t
Triceratops	5.4 t
Tyrannosaurus	6.4 t
Ultrasaurus	130 t

2. Which dinosaur is the heaviest? the lightest?

3. Would all the students in your class have as great a mass as any of the dinosaurs?
What about all the students in your school? Which dinosaurs?

4. Trucks with a total mass of more than 36 000 kg are not allowed on some highways. Which of the dinosaurs wouldn't be allowed on these highways?

5. What else do you think might be measured in tonnes?

Take Your Pick

ELEVATORS

About how many tonnes can this elevator safely hold?

each person weighs
85 kg

MAXIMUM
16 occupants

CUPBOARD SPACE

Estimate the volume of the largest cupboard in your classroom.

BASE TEN STRUCTURES

Use base ten blocks to build several different structures with a volume of 200 cm^3.
How high a structure can you build?

MAKING BOXES

Use centimetre grid paper. Cut out a 10 cm by 6 cm rectangle. Then cut one square out of each corner and fold to make an open box.

How many centimetre cubes will it hold? Then cut three more squares out of each corner and fold to make an open box.

How many centimetre cubes will that box hold? Which open box has the greater volume?

TWICE AS BIG

This solid is made with centimetre cubes. What is its volume?

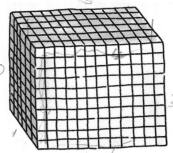

Another rectangular prism has a volume that is twice this. How long might its sides be?

Make up the other problems. Post them on the bulletin board for your classmates to solve.

Solving a Problem by Acting It Out

Try this problem before going on.

WATER LILY

The queen-size royal water lily in Brazil has leaves that are over 2 m across. About how many students can stand on a surface this size?

Art's group solved the problem by acting it out.

We made a cross with four metre sticks and a circle with string.

Then we removed the metre sticks and crowded our classmates into the circle.

Finish their work.

Work in a group.

Solve these problems by acting them out.

SHARING MASSES

One student is holding four 10 kg masses. Another student is holding four 5 kg masses. A third student is holding five 2 kg masses. A fourth student is holding six 1 kg masses. Can they share the masses so that each holds the same amount? If so, how?

ADDING ON

One student adds 1 cube to this solid. Each of 9 other students adds 2 more cubes to it than the student before. What will the volume of the solid be when all of the students have added their cubes?

HANDSHAKES

Six friends meet. Each shakes hands with each of the others. How many handshakes are there?

Practising What You've Learned

1. Name something you might measure in each unit.

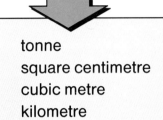

tonne
square centimetre
cubic metre
kilometre
cubic centimetre
square metre

2. Estimate the distance between Kenora and Thunder Bay.

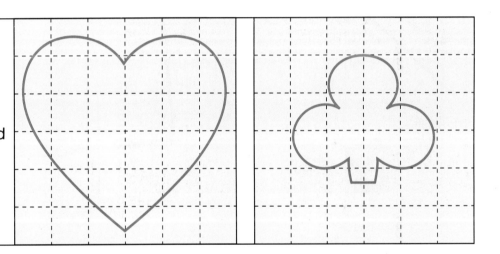

Scale 1 cm represents 50 km

3. Estimate the area of the first shape one way. Then estimate the area of the second shape a different way.

4. Make another rectangle with the same area but a greater perimeter.

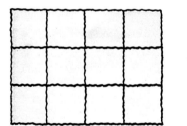

5. What is the volume of this solid made from centimetre cubes?

Make another shape with the same volume. Draw or describe it.

6. Which is more? Tell why.

- $40 \, m^2$ or $4000 \, cm^2$
- $2 \, t$ or $2000 \, kg$
- $5 \, m^3$ or $500 \, cm^3$

7. Make a net for an open box that takes $20 \, cm^3$ of space.

133

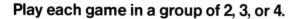

Play each game in a group of 2, 3, or 4.

How High?

- Shuffle the base cards. Place them face down in a pile.
- Roll 2 dice to create a 2-digit number. The digits can be in either order.
- Take that number of cubes.
- Turn over a base card.
- Imagine a structure built on that base with the cubes you have.
- Estimate how many cubes high the structure would be at its tallest point.
- Build the structure to check your estimate.
- Score 1 point for being within 1 cube of the height,
    2 points for being the exact height.
- Take turns.
- The winner is the first player to reach a score of 10.

Example

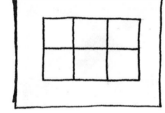 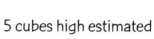

25 used   5 cubes high estimated   Score 2 points.

Last One In

- Roll a die to get an area from 1 square unit to 6 square units.
- Color a shape with that area on a 10 by 10 grid.
- Take turns coloring shapes. Each player uses a different color.
- The winner is the last player to be able to color a shape.

Example

      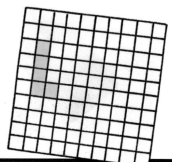

PACKING CARTONS

What size of box can be made to hold exactly 8 of these cartons?

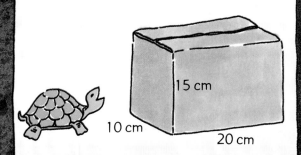

15 cm

10 cm

20 cm

CUTTING PAPER

Is the perimeter of half a sheet of paper $\frac{1}{2}$ of the perimeter of a whole sheet? Explain.

Would the perimeter of a third of a sheet of paper be $\frac{1}{3}$ of the perimeter of a whole sheet?

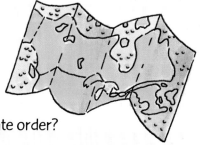

CANADA

Use a map of Canada.

For each province, trace the outline and cut it out.
Order the provinces from least to greatest area.
Why might tracing some provinces from one map
and others from a different map not result in an accurate order?

CLASSROOM SPACE

About how many square metres of floor are in your classroom? What about cubic metres of air? Compare the floor area and the volume of your classroom with another room in your school.

CRACKERS

How many boxes are needed to have one tonne of crackers? Would that many boxes fit in your classroom? Explain.

FRISCUITS

250 g

Make up the other problems. Post them on the bulletin board for your classmates to solve.

1. Which is the most reasonable measurement for the area of a living room window?

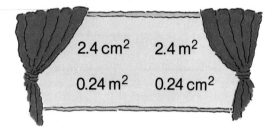

2.4 cm² 2.4 m²

0.24 m² 0.24 cm²

2. Rewrite the signs using kilograms and metres. Why are larger units useful?

LOAD LIMIT 16 t

KAMLOOPS 185 km

3. What unit would you most likely use to measure the volume of a bar of soap? a refrigerator?
What unit would you use to measure the mass of each?

4. This garden is 8 m by 3 m.
What is the scale of this diagram?
What is the garden's area? perimeter?

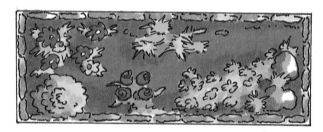

Could a different garden have
• the same perimeter, but more area? Explain.
• the same area, but more perimeter? Explain.

5. Find the area of this kite. Tell how you did it.

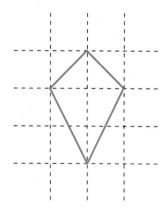

A rectangle has an area 20 times as great as this kite. Sketch a rectangle and show the side lengths possible.

6. A rectangular prism has a volume of 40 cm³. Make a model.
Draw a net on grid paper of an open box with the same volume.
Make a model of a rectangular prism with a volume $\frac{1}{8}$ of this volume.

Thinking Back

Use two rectangles. Show why the rectangle with the greater area is not necessarily the one with the greater perimeter.

Explain to someone two different methods you might use to find the area of the sole of your foot.

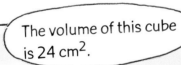

What would you name a distance of 1000 km? Why? Is such a unit useful?

The volume of this cube is 24 cm^2.

Tell two things that are wrong with this statement.

How would you determine the number of math books needed to make a mass of one tonne?

What questions do you still have about measurement?

Examining

▼ What number is shown?

Use base ten blocks. Compared to this number, show a number that is
- 1000 less
- 2000 greater
- twice as great
- half as great

▼ What number is shown in the row of blocks? in the array of blocks?

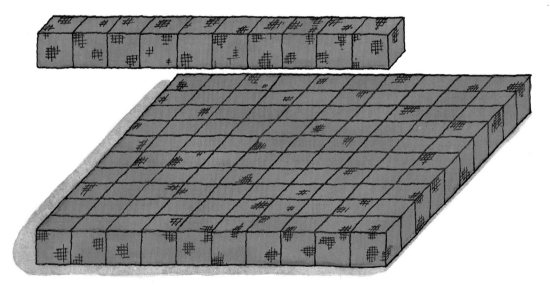

What if there were 2 layers of the array?   10 layers of the array?

◀ Why do you think millimetre and millilitre
both start with *milli*?
What do you think *milli* means?
What other words do you know that start with *milli*?

Large Numbers

▶ How many bills would this be if the prize was all in $1000 bills? $100 bills? $10 bills?

THIS IS TO CERTIFY THAT ZOE PLOUSOS WON $100 000

To claim your prize, read the instructions that follow.

▼ This square has 100 dots.

Estimate how many dots like this would cover this page.

What is the greatest number you have ever seen written?
What did the number tell about?

PRINCE RUPERT 148 km

NEW TOWN HOMES FROM $129 000   REAL ESTATE NEWS

40 000 FANS AT SKYDOME WATCH THE BLUE JAYS WORLD SERIES   SPORTS

ST. JOHN'S Pop. 96 200

Two of the digits in a 3-digit number are 6 and 7.
The number is a multiple of 3. What could it be?

Collecting Pop Can Tabs

Caroline's Guide company collects pop can tabs. They put 100 tabs in a small bag. Then they put 10 small bags in a large bag.

How many tabs are in a large bag?

What base ten block represents the number of tabs in a small bag? in a large bag?

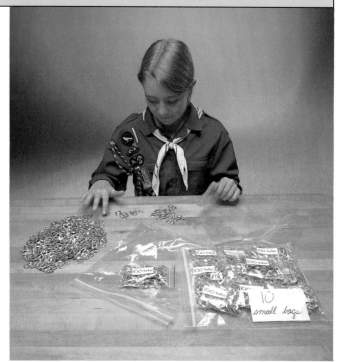

This model shows how many tabs Caroline's company collected.

thousands	hundreds	tens	ones

1. How many tabs did they collect?
   How many large bags do they have? small bags not in large bags? leftover tabs?

Model using base ten blocks.

2. Another Guide company collected 3456 tabs. Model this.
   How many large bags do they have? small bags not in large bags? leftover tabs?

3. Another Guide company has 7 large bags, 3 small bags, and some leftover tabs. How many tabs altogether might this company have? Model that number.

4. How many large bags are needed for 10 000 tabs?
   How can you show 10 000 using base ten blocks?
   Do these three companies have 10 000 tabs?

140

Work in a group.

Model using base ten blocks.

5. How many tabs has each Scout troop collected? Which troop has collected the most tabs? How can you tell?

1st Pickering Scout Troop

2nd Pickering Scout Troop

3rd Pickering Scout Troop

6. The 3rd Pickering Troop gets two more tabs. What can they do now?

7. About how many tabs have all three troops collected?

8. Ten large bags are put in a box. How many tabs are in a box? How would you model that number?

9. A row of 10 large cubes is sometimes called a big long. A 10 by 10 array of large cubes is sometimes called a big flat. How many tabs would a big flat represent?

10. This model shows the number of tabs one Guide district collected. How many tabs does this represent? Write a number that shows
   • 10 000 more tabs
   • 100 000 more tabs

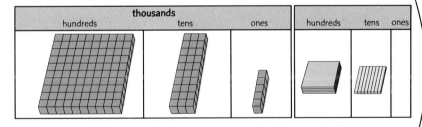

11. One Guide company collected this many tabs. How many is this?

The number of tabs collected by a Scout troop has the same 5 digits but in a different order.
Could they have collected more than 30 000?   less than 10 000?

12. Do you know any Guide, Scout, or other groups that collect pop can tabs? Why do they collect them?

141

Raining Pennies

Estimating a million

The street was covered with pennies. There must have been a million of them, two million maybe or even more, three million, four, five million shiny, bright, sparkling, new pennies. A midnight money van came down the street, and it stopped right in front of the house. The driver got out, and he began to sweep up the pennies. Matthew ran outside.

"It's been raining money!" he cried.

from *Matthew and the Midnight Money Van* by Allen Morgan

A million is 1000 thousand.
How would you write the numeral?
Write the numerals for the other numbers in the paragraph.
How many thousands is each?

Work with a partner.

Write your answers using numerals.

1. In the story, the midnight money man suggested that he and Matthew could split the pennies fifty-fifty. What is meant by fifty-fifty? What is each share if there are 1 million pennies?

2. What is 1 000 000 pennies equal to in $1 coins? $10 bills? $100 bills? $1000 bills?

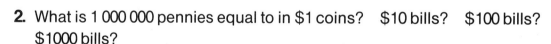

3. In the story, the midnight turkeys flipped pennies and called out "heads" or "tails." How many pennies would you expect to turn up heads if you flipped 2 million pennies? 3 million pennies? Why?

4. How could this help you calculate the length of 100 pennies? 1000 pennies? 10 000 pennies? 100 000 pennies? 1 000 000 pennies?

How many kilometres long would a line of 1 000 000 pennies be?

5. This square contains 100 pennies. How many squares like this is a million pennies?
Would a million pennies fit on the top of your table? on the classroom floor? Explain.

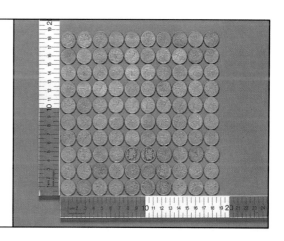

6. Answer one of these questions. How would you estimate
- how high a stack of one million pennies would be? Do you think you could stack pennies that high?
- how many jars you would need to hold 1 million pennies?
- how heavy 1 000 000 pennies are?

7. If you rolled 1 million pennies, how many rolls would you have?
What would you do if you had 1 000 000 pennies?

10 coins are worth 72¢. What could they be?

Counting People

Reading, writing, and comparing

The Eight Largest Cities in Canada

Calgary, AB	723 300
Edmonton, AB	827 700
Montréal, PQ	3 068 100
Ottawa, ON	651 900
Québec, PQ	622 200
Toronto, ON	3 751 700
Winnipeg, MB	647 100
Vancouver, BC	1 547 000

The population of Montréal is three million, sixty-eight thousand, one hundred. Read the populations of Calgary and Vancouver. How are the digits grouped? Why do you think they are grouped?

1. Which city's population is shown in this place value chart? Show the populations of two other cities.

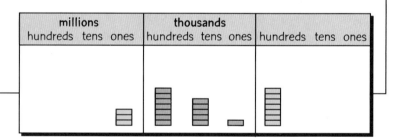

Work with a partner.

2. List the cities in order from greatest to least population. Did you find some comparisons easier than others? Explain.

3. Which cities' populations would be rounded up when rounded to the nearest hundred thousand? Round each population to the nearest hundred thousand.

4. The population of Hamilton, ON is five hundred ninety-four thousand, six hundred. Where do you think it ranks? Why?

5. Do you think the populations are exact numbers? Explain.

144

Take Your Pick

COUNTING WORDS

Do you think you have ever read a book with a million words? About how many pages would be in a paperback novel with 1 000 000 words?

REDEEMING COUPONS

On an average day, Canadians redeem 679 452 coupons. If the average value of a coupon is 50¢, about how much money is saved on an average day?

FORWARD AND BACKWARD

The digits in 123 456 are in order.
The digits in 87 654 are in order when read backward.
How many 6-digit numbers can be written with their digits in order either forward or backward? How many 5-digit numbers could be written this way?

ONES AND NINES

Each digit in a 7-digit number is either a 1 or 9.
What is the number if it is as close as possible to 1 000 000? 2 000 000? To which million did you get closer? How much closer?

ZEROS

How many numbers between 100 000 and 200 000 end in a 0?

Make up other problems. Post them on the bulletin board for your classmates to solve.

How many blue bags would balance one yellow bag?

Examining Our Diet

On an average day, Canadians eat
- 275 669 kg of butter
- 300 639 kg of cheddar cheese
- 197 764 kg of processed cheese
- 84 898 kg of cottage cheese
- 142 295 kg of fresh broccoli
  (about 620 000 bunches)
- 226 378 kg of fresh mushrooms
- 80 849 kg of peanut butter
- 274 888 kg of chocolate
- 284 932 kg of potato chips

Peter is estimating the number of kilograms of cheddar and processed cheese eaten on an average day.

Finish his estimate. Is it high or low? Explain.

What other numbers could you have used to estimate? Can you add them in your head?

cheddar cheese
300 639 is a bit over 300 thousand

processed cheese
197 764 is almost 198 thousand

Kate is estimating how many more kilograms of butter than peanut butter are eaten on an average day.

Finish her estimate. Is it high or low? Explain.

What other numbers could you have used to estimate?
Can you subtract them in your head?

butter
275 669 is a bit over 275 thousand

peanut butter
80 849 is a bit over 80 thousand
20 + 100 + 75 =

146

Use the data about what Canadians eat.

1. On an average day, about how many more kilograms are eaten of
   - processed cheese than cottage cheese?
   - mushrooms than broccoli?
   - cheddar cheese than butter?

2. On an average day, about how many kilograms of chocolate and potato chips are eaten?
   Of which is more eaten? About how much more?

3. How would you estimate the number of kilograms of cottage cheese eaten in one week?
   Estimate the number of kilograms of any one of the cheeses eaten
   - in a week
   - in a month
   Are your estimates high or low? Explain.

4. Peter is estimating how many bunches of broccoli are in 1 kg.

   Since 142 295 kg of broccoli is about 620 000 bunches, 150 thousand kg is more than 600 thousand bunches.

   Why did he use these numbers?
   Finish his estimate. Is it high or low? Explain.

5. About how many days does it take Canadians to eat 1 000 000 kg of mushrooms?   broccoli?

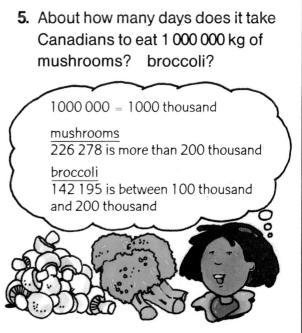

   1 000 000 = 1000 thousand

   mushrooms
   226 278 is more than 200 thousand

   broccoli
   142 195 is between 100 thousand and 200 thousand

6. How many grams of potato chips are eaten on an average day?
   About how many grams are eaten, on average, by each of the almost 28 million Canadians? About what fraction of a kilogram is this?

7. On an average day, Canadians drink 7 764 385 L of milk. About how many glasses is that?
   If most milk drinkers drink 3 glasses a day, about how many milk drinkers would that be?

8. Make up 3 problems about the data for another group to solve.

9. How do you think this data might have been gathered?

What division might have been done?

Going to School Around the World

Country	Number of Elementary		
	Schools	Teachers	Students
Australia	8 442	108 253	1 687 390
Canada	9 307	163 914	3 493 841
England	24 609	208 700	4 550 300
Japan	24 901	445 000	9 872 000
Mexico	80 518	455 693	14 875 000
United States	71 608	1 517 000	31 704 000

Fran is calculating how many more students than teachers there are in Canada.

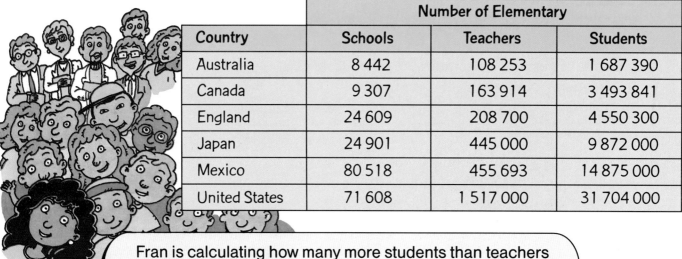

First she estimates.

3 493 841 is almost 3500 thousand
163 914 is almost 200 thousand
3500 thousand − 200 thousand = 3300 thousand

Then she calculates.

$$3 \quad 4 \quad 9 \quad 3 \quad 8 \quad 4 \quad 1 \quad - \quad 1 \quad 6 \quad 3 \quad 9 \quad 1 \quad 4 \quad =$$

Why did she estimate before using the calculator?

Work with a partner.

Estimate and then calculate.

1. How many more students than teachers are there in England? in Japan?

2. In North America, what is the total number of schools? teachers?

3. How many times as many students as teachers are there in Australia? in Japan?

4. What operation do you use to find average? Find the average number of teachers in a school for any three countries. Order these countries from most to least average number of teachers.

5. Make up two problems about the data for another group to solve.

Take Your Pick

IMMIGRATION

Number of Immigrants to Canada in a Typical Day

European	142
African	37
Australasian	7
Asian	304
North and Central American	70
South American	24

About how many immigrants come to Canada in a year?
About half of the immigrants settle in Ontario.
About how many is that?

SLINKYS

One million Slinkys
are sold in Canada in
4 years.
About how many are
sold each day?

MULTIPLICATION

If you multiply a 6-digit number by a 3-digit number,
how many digits are likely in the product? Explain.

MONEY, MONEY, MONEY

On an average day, the Royal Canadian
Mint mints

509 589	$1 coins
567	50¢ coins
326 027	quarters
542 466	dimes
386 301	nickels
2 928 767	pennies

About how many dollars would all
these coins be worth?

NINES

How could you use a calculator to find
99 999 × 99 999?

**Make up other problems. Post them
on the bulletin board for your
classmates to solve.**

Solving a Problem by Finding Needed Information

Try this problem before going on.

BUYING MONEY

How many Russian rubles can you buy with $300 Canadian?

Pat's group solved this problem by finding needed information.

We called a bank to find out the exchange rate.
We learned that $1 Canadian buys 333 Russian rubles.

$1 buys 333 rubles
So $300 buys   333 × 300 rubles
              = 99 900 rubles

How many Canadian dollars would it take to be a Russian millionaire?

Work in a group.

Solve these problems by first finding the needed information.

RAISINS

About how many individual serving boxes do you need to get one million raisins?

TO AND FROM

About how many times would you have to travel to and from school to cover the average distance between the moon and Earth?

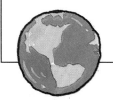

COUNTING CANADIANS

How often are people living in Canada officially counted? What is this called? What was the change in population of each province between the last two official counts? Which province had the greatest change? the least?

1. Write each number in words.   120 000   1 200 000   100 200

2. Write each number as a numeral.
- two million
- three hundred thousand
- one million, three hundred twenty thousand, twenty-four

3. How many thousands of dollars is each week's sales?

February Sales

Week 1	$20 000
Week 2	$1 200 000
Week 3	$314 000
Week 4	$234 000

4. What is 3 000 000 in
- hundred thousands?
- thousands?
- tens?

5. Order these numbers from least to greatest.

3 214 013   43 125

32 513.8   40 012

6. Can you walk 1 000 000 mm? Explain.

7. Find the next three numbers in the pattern.

213 567   314 567   415 567

8. A baseball player signed a contract to be paid $3 500 000 over 2 years.
If he plays about 150 games each year, about how much does he earn for each game?
If he comes up to bat about 4 times each game, about how much does he earn for each time at bat?

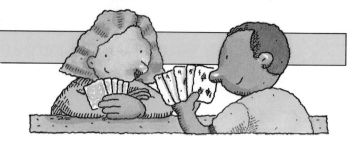

Play each game in a group of 2, 3, or 4.

Deal Numbers

- Remove the face cards and aces from a deck of playing cards.
- Shuffle the cards and deal 6 to each player.
- Form the greatest 6-digit number possible using your cards.
- Then score, depending on your number,
  1 point if it is even
  2 points if it is a multiple of 5
  3 points if it is greater than 700 000
  5 points if it rounds to 500 000
- Play until one player has 25 points.

Example

855 432	even	1 point
	> 700 000	3 points
		Score 4 points

Variations:
- Make the least number possible.
- Change the scoring.

Limit 10 000

- Remove the face cards and aces from a deck of playing cards.
- Shuffle the cards and deal one card face up to each player.
- Then deal one card at a time, face up, to each player until the player says to stop.
- Say stop when you estimate that the product of your numbers is close to, but not greater than, 10 000.
- When all players have said stop, use a calculator to check each multiplication.
- The player closest to 10 000 but not greater than scores 5 points.
- Continue until one player has 25 points.

Example

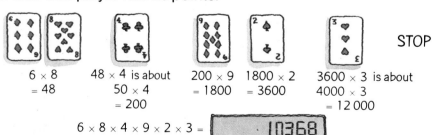

6×8	48×4 is about	200×9	1800×2	3600×3 is about
$= 48$	50×4	$= 1800$	$= 3600$	4000×3
	$= 200$			$= 12\,000$

$6 \times 8 \times 4 \times 9 \times 2 \times 3 =$ [10368]

Variation: Use a different number, such as 50 000.

Take Your Pick

SUM AND DIFFERENCE

Use any digits except 0 to form two numbers with a sum close to 900 000 and a difference close to 200 000. Find another pair of numbers.

HOW OLD?

Are you older than one million seconds? Explain.

CANADIAN FAMILIES

Number of Children	Number of Families (to the nearest thousand)
1	1 770 000
2	1 821 000
3	699 000
4	182 000
5	41 000
6	12 000
7	4 000
8	3 000

About how many families have
• 5 or more children?
• 2 or 3 children?
• 1 or more children?
About how many times as many children have one brother or sister as children who have three brothers or sisters?

EVENS AND ODDS

The red squares must be even digits. The blue squares must be odd digits. What number is as close as possible to 500 000?

CALCULATOR PATTERN

Investigate this pattern. Predict the next product.

1×2
11×22
111×222

Make up other problems. Post them on the bulletin board for your classmates to solve.

1. Write a numeral for
   - a number between 500 thousand and 1 million
   - a number a little greater than 243 thousand

2. Use the digits from 1 to 6 to create a number less than 600 000 but greater than 530 000.

3. A number less than 300 000 is subtracted from a number greater than 800 000. What do you know about the difference?

4. In Canada, there are
   51 966 doctors,
   250 458 nurses,
   1 226 hospitals.

   How many times as many nurses are there as doctors? doctors are there as hospitals?

5. An ice cream sundae made in Edmonton in 1988 had a mass of 24 908 kg. It contained

   20 270.7 kg of ice cream,
   4 394.4 kg of syrup,
   234.7 kg of topping.

   How much more syrup was there than topping? How many grams of topping were there?

6. How many $20 bills are equal to $1 000 000?
   How do you know?

7. A square has an area of 1 000 000 cm². What is the length of each side in centimetres? metres? kilometres?

Thinking Back

When might you need to subtract two 6-digit numbers to find an exact answer? When would an estimate do? Explain.

Do you think there is a greatest number? Why or why not?

Read this poem.

One Million

1 000 000 pennies, they say,
is 1000 thousand.
1 000 000 pennies, I say,
would be really great pay.
1 000 000 pennies, they say,
is 10 000 hundred.
1 000 000 pennies, I say,
would be really great pay.

by Elaine Mullen

Write a poem about a large number.

When have you seen a million of something? Tell about it.

When might 1000 of something be greater in some way than 1 000 000 of something else?

1 000   1 000 000

What questions do you still have about large numbers?

9 Introducing Probability

▼ When one die is rolled, which result is impossible? certain? likely?
- either an odd number or an even number
- a number greater than 6
- a number less than 5

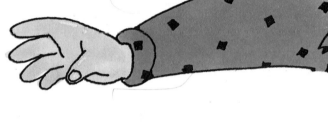

▼ Which is more likely to happen when a coin is tossed 100 times? Explain.

- always heads
- always tails
- heads about $\frac{1}{4}$ of the time
- tails about $\frac{1}{2}$ of the time

◄ A new boy joins your class. Which prediction about him is most likely to be true? Why?
- His birthday is March 21.
- He is 10 years old.
- He has 7 brothers and 5 sisters.
- His name is Fred.

and Statistics

◀ Explain how you could find the average number in each pile without calculating.

▼ Which statements are true about the average height of this family?
- less than 160 cm
- between 120 cm and 140 cm
- less than 120 cm

Use the phrase *"the average is about"* to describe
- the age of the students in your class
- the number of students in the classes at your school
- the length of pencils used by students in your class

160 cm   100 cm   ~~140 cm~~   ~~120 cm~~

120 cm   140 cm

How many cubes are needed to build this cube?
What numbers of cubes can be used to build larger cubes?
What do you notice about these numbers?

Playing Baseball

Eryn either strikes out or hits a home run each time she is at bat. One outcome is as likely as the other.

Predict how many home runs and strikeouts she will likely have after 10 times at bat.

Bram is doing an experiment to simulate Eryn's performance at bat.
He writes SO on one slip of paper and HR on another.
Then he put the slips in a bowl.
He draws one slip, records the result, and puts the slip back in the bowl.
He does this 10 times.

1. How does your prediction compare with Bram's results?

Work with a partner.

2. Simulate Eryn's performance like Bram did.
   Compare your results
   • to Bram's
   • to those of 3 other pairs of students
   Tell what you notice.

3. Josh either strikes out or hits a home run. He strikes out twice as often as he hits a home run. Which set of slips should you use to simulate his performance at bat?

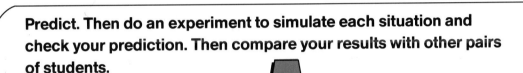

Predict. Then do an experiment to simulate each situation and check your prediction. Then compare your results with other pairs of students.

4. How many home runs and strikeouts will Josh likely have after 10 times at bat?

5. How many times at bat will Josh likely need to have 3 strikeouts in a row? What about Eryn?

6. Jesse either walks, strikes out, or hits a home run. How many home runs will she likely hit after 20 times at bat in each situation?

Example 1

Example 2

Example 3

For each situation, describe how likely each outcome is.

7. Use any of these outcomes and 5 slips of paper. You do not have to use all the outcomes.
How often will a player likely walk after 20 times at bat?
W (walk)   SO (strikeout)   HR (home run)

Find this sum.
696 + 986 + 686 + 818 + 969 + 919
Turn your book upside down and add the
numbers you now see. What do you notice?

Predicting Weather in Chewandswallow
Using fractions to describe chance

In the land of Chewandswallow,
it never rained rain. It never
snowed snow. And it never blew
just wind. It rained things like
soup and juice. It snowed mashed
potatoes and green peas. And
sometimes the wind blew in
storms of hamburgers.

from *Cloudy with a Chance of
Meatballs* by Judi Barrett
and Ron Barrett

You can simulate
the weather by doing
an experiment.

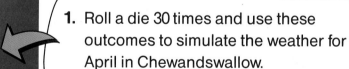

Work in a group.

**Use grid paper to record your results for a 30-day month.
Compare your answers with other groups.**

1. Roll a die 30 times and use these
outcomes to simulate the weather for
April in Chewandswallow.

- An even number is pancakes.
- An odd number is syrup.

How many days did it snow pancakes?
rain syrup?

What fraction of the days did it snow
pancakes? rain syrup?

2. Which fraction best describes the
probability of snowing pancakes in
April? Why?

$\frac{1}{30}$ $\qquad$ $\frac{1}{10}$ $\qquad$ $\frac{1}{5}$ $\qquad$ $\frac{1}{2}$

3. If the weather was similar to April for the entire year, about how many days would it likely snow pancakes?

4. Roll a die 30 times and use these outcomes to simulate the weather for June in Chewandswallow.
  · A number greater than 1 is spaghetti.
  · A number greater than 2 is meat sauce.
  · The number 6 is grated cheese.

How many days did it rain spaghetti? meat sauce? grated cheese? all three foods? no food?

What fraction tells the probability of raining spaghetti? meat sauce? grated cheese? all three foods? no food?

5. Roll a die 30 times and use these outcomes to simulate the weather for September in Chewandswallow.
  · An even number is hamburger patties.
  · A multiple of 3 is buns.
  · The number 2 is ketchup.

What fraction tells the probability of raining hamburger patties? buns? ketchup? hamburger patties and buns? no food?

Why is raining hamburger patties more probable than raining ketchup?

Why is raining all three foods impossible?

6. Choose a food that you like and one that you don't like. Make up a probability rule for one die so that more days in November will rain the food you like than the one you don't like. Simulate the weather to check.

Hours of TV Watched in One Week

Gabe	☐☐☐☐☐☐☐
Doreen	☐☐☐
Jonah	☐☐☐☐☐☐☐☐
Rachel	☐☐☐☐☐☐☐☐☐☐

One ☐ represents 2 h.

Make up 5 questions about the pictograph for a classmate to answer.

How does your TV viewing compare with this data?

Choosing a Student

Calculating theoretical probabilities

One student is needed to take the hamsters home for the holidays.
Ten students volunteer.
The class decides to write each volunteer's name on a slip of paper.
The volunteer whose name is chosen gets to take care of the hamsters.

Why does each name have an equal chance of being chosen?

By calculating, the probability of choosing a name starting with A is $\frac{1}{2}$ because 5 out of 10 names start with A.

$$\frac{5}{10} = \frac{1}{2}$$

1. Calculate the probability of choosing Anna. Explain.

Work in a group.

2. Calculate the probability of choosing a name starting with

    B   D   J   R

4. Put the slips in a container and mix them up. Draw a slip, record the result in a tally chart, and return the slip to the container.
Do this 50 times. How do the results of the experiment compare with the calculated probability?

3. Write the first name of each student in your group on a slip of paper.
Calculate the probability of choosing
• your name
• a name with more than 5 letters

5. List the first names of the students in your class. Calculate the probability of choosing a name that
• begins with a letter from A to M
• has at least 2 letters
• begins with a vowel
• has an even number of letters

BOARD GAMES

In some board games, you get an extra turn by rolling a double with a pair of dice.
Predict the probability of rolling a double.
Roll a pair of dice 30 times. Check your prediction.

PHONE NUMBER DIGITS

List the phone numbers of 10 students in your class.
Calculate the probability of choosing a phone number containing

- a 0
- 7 digits
- all different digits

CHOOSE A SPINNER

Which spinner was most likely used to get this result from 10 spins? Explain.
Is it possible to get this result using the other spinners?

Red	Blue
⊮⊮ IIII	I

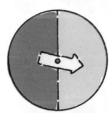 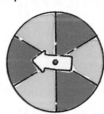 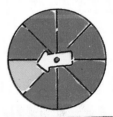

SAMPLING CANDIES

About what fraction of the candies in the bin are likely yellow?
What is the probability of choosing a blue candy from the bin?
Could there be more than 4 colors in the bin?
Explain.

Color of Candies Taken from Bin

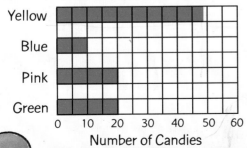

PLAYING HEADSY

In the game of Headsy, you get 2 points for tossing a Head and 1 point for a Tail. The first player to get more than 30 points wins.

Predict how many turns a player might need to win.

Do an experiment to check your prediction.

Make up other problems. Post them on the bulletin board for your classmates to solve.

Use your calculator. Complete this multiplication sentence using each of the other digits from 1 to 9 once.

☐38 × ☐☐ = ☐☐☐6

Examining Comic Strips

Dolores made this graph.

Which statements are true? Explain.

The average number of letters in these titles is
- between 2 and 19
- close to 10
- close to 5
- close to 15

Number of Letters in Comic Strip Titles

	1	2	3	4	5	6	7	8	9	10	11	12	13	14	15	16	17	18	19	20
Peanuts	○	○	○	○	○	○	○													
Garfield	○	○	○	○	○	○	○	○												
Blondie	○	○	○	○	○	○	○													
Andy Capp	●	○	●	○	●	●	●	○												
B.C.	●	○																		
Calvin and Hobbes	●	●	●	●	●	●	●	●	●	●	●	●	●	●	●	●				
Wizard of Id	○	○	○	●	○	○	○	○												
Kaleb	○	○	○	○	○															
Sally Forth	●	●	●	○	●	●	●	●	○	○										
For Better or For Worse	○	○	○	○	○	○		○	○	○	○	○		○	○	○	○	○	○	○

Number of Letters

Number of Letters in Comic Strip Titles

	1	2	3	4	5	6	7	8	9	10	11	12	13	14	15	16	17	18	19	20
Peanuts	○	○	○	○	○	○	○	○	○											
Garfield	○	○	○	○	○	○	○	○	○											
Blondie	○	○	○	○	○	○	○	○	○											
Andy Capp	●	○	●	○	●	●	●	○	○											
B.C.	○	○	○	○	○	●	●	●	●											
Calvin and Hobbes	●	●	●	●	●	●	●	●	●											
Wizard of Id	○	○	○	○	○	○	○	○	○											
Kaleb	○	○	○	○	○	●	●	○	○											
Sally Forth	●	●	●	●	●	○	●	●	○											
For Better or For Worse	○	○	○	○	○	○	○	○	○											

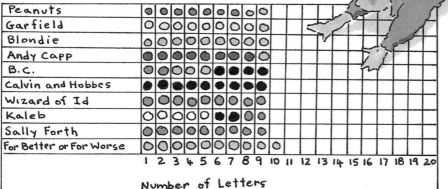

Number of Letters

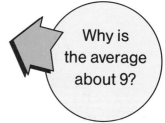

Dolores rearranged the counters to make each comic strip show about the same number of letters.

Why is the average about 9?

Work in a group.

Use at least 6 comic strips from a newspaper. Answer 4 of the following questions.

What is the average number, to the nearest whole number, of

1. different characters?   **2.** sections?   **3.** speech balloons?

4. words?   **5.** punctuation marks?   **6.** pictures of animals?

If all the page numbers in this book were multiplied together, what would the ones digit be?

Remembering Trivia

What Trivia Do You Remember?

Each statement is true or false.

1. A $5 bill is blue.
2. A dollar coin has 11 sides.
3. Q is the only letter missing from a telephone keyboard or dial.
4. A schooner or sailing ship is on one side of a dime.
5. The top light of a traffic light is green.
6. A YIELD sign is diamond shaped.
7. 1 is opposite 5 on a die.
8. The Queen faces right on any coin.
9. A STOP sign has 6 sides.
10. A deck of playing cards has exactly 50 cards.

Here are the scores for 5 students.

Jason	6
Arlene	3
Ian	3
Mark	2
Jackie	6

Mark calculated the average.
Check this by graphing.

$$\frac{6 + 3 + 3 + 2 + 6}{5} = \frac{20}{5} = 4$$

Work in a group.

Each person should answer the quiz without any help.

1. Calculate the average score of your group to the nearest whole number.

2. Compare the average score of your group to those of other groups.
How can you find the average score of all students in the class?

3. Add 2 to each score of your group. Find the new average.
Compare this average to your first average. Tell what you notice.

4. How can you tell without calculating which group had the greatest average score?

    5, 5, 5, 6, 6

    10, 7, 7, 7, 6   10, 10, 10, 7, 6

5. The average score of this group is 5. What might the missing numbers be?

    4   4   ?   ?

6. Make up 6 different scores for the quiz that would have an average of 5.

7. Why might your teacher want to know the average score on a test?

Take Your Pick

IN BETWEEN

What might be the missing number if the average of the 5 numbers is between 10 and 15?

5 6 7 8 ?

CONSECUTIVE NUMBERS

What do you notice about the average of 3 consecutive numbers like 98, 99, and 100? Find the average of 4 different consecutive numbers, then 5, and then 6.
Compare the results. Tell what you notice.

2 3 4 5 6 7 8

EQUALIZING AVERAGES

What is the unknown mass if the average mass of the first group equals the average mass of the second group?

| 10 kg | 12 kg | 14 kg | ? kg |

| 12 kg | 14 kg | 16 kg | 18 kg |

CHANGING NUMBERS

Use your calculator to find the average of 90, 93, 100, and 117.
Add the same even number to 2 of the 4 numbers.
Find the new average.
Compare it with the first average.
Tell what you notice.

AVERAGE DIE

Predict the average number when a die is rolled 12 times. Do an experiment to test your prediction.

Make up other problems. Post them on the bulletin board for your classmates to solve.

166

Solving a Problem by Drawing a Diagram

Try this problem before going on.

THE PROBABILITY IS . . .

For this pair of spinners, calculate the probability of getting
- a sum of 6
- the same number on both spinners

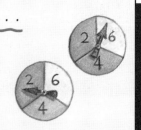

Shauna's group solved the problem by drawing a tree diagram.

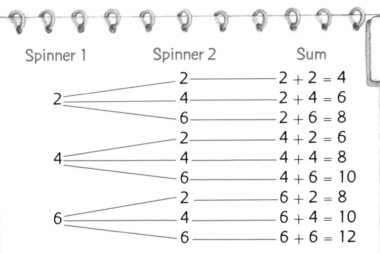

Spinner 1	Spinner 2	Sum
2	2	2 + 2 = 4
	4	2 + 4 = 6
	6	2 + 6 = 8
4	2	4 + 2 = 6
	4	4 + 4 = 8
	6	4 + 6 = 10
6	2	6 + 2 = 8
	4	6 + 4 = 10
	6	6 + 6 = 12

First we need to find all the possible outcomes.

2 out of the 9 possible outcomes give a sum of 6.

The probability of getting a sum of 6 is $\frac{2}{9}$.

3 out of the 9 possible outcomes show the same number on both spinners.

Finish their work.

Then calculate the probability of getting a sum of

10   12   14

Work in a group.

Solve these problems by drawing a tree diagram.

SPEAKING NUMBERS

Two students each say a number from 1 to 4. Calculate the probability that they will both say the same number.

SWITCH POSITIONS

How many different ways can the 3 light switches be positioned?

Calculate the probability that they will all be ON.

TOSSING DICE

How many sums can be tossed with a pair of dice? Calculate the probability of getting a sum of

2   6   7   10

Why do you think 7 is considered a lucky number?

Practising What You've Learned

1. Predict how many times the printing on a hexagonal pencil will be on the bottom when the pencil is rolled 24 times. Do an experiment to check your prediction.

2. Design a colored spinner where the probability of spinning blue is

   $\frac{1}{2}$ $\frac{1}{4}$ 1   0

3. Each coin of play money was tossed 1000 times.
   Which coin is probably not a fair one?

H	T		H	T
8	992		495	505

4. Calculate the probability of spinning an even number.

5. Show how to use the graph to find the average length of the ski trails.

   Cross Country Ski Trails

Meadow View	
Pine Valley	
Evergreen Alley	
Deer	
Hill Top	
Jack Rabbit	

   Each ⬜ represents 1 km.

6. A card is picked from a deck of playing cards. Which prediction about the card has the greatest chance of being correct? Explain.

   It's a diamond.   It's a Jack.   It's the Jack of diamonds.

7. List any 4 different numbers that have an average of 7.

8. Which set of numbers has the greater average? Explain.

   5, 6, 7, 8, 20   5, 6, 7, 8, 100

9. The average price of 4 marking pens is $1. But not one pen costs exactly $1. Does this seem reasonable? Explain.

10. What sums are possible using this pair of spinners?

    Would you say *impossible*, *certain*, or *likely* to describe the probability that the sum is
    an even number?   an odd number?
    less than 16?   equal to 7, 9, or 11?

Playing Games for Practice

Play each game in a group of 3 or 4.

Making Choices

- Player 1 rolls a die 3 times and finds the sum.
- The other players take turns predicting whether they will roll a sum greater than, less than, or equal to the first sum rolled.
- After predicting, the players roll and test their predictions.
- Score 1 point to each player making a correct prediction
  - 1 point to Player 1 for each other player's incorrect prediction
- Take turns being Player 1. The first player to reach 10 points wins.

Example

Player 1	Player 2	Player 3
	Prediction: greater than 13	Prediction: less than 13
		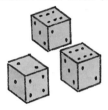
Sum = 13	Sum = 10	Sum = 14
Score 2 points (because Players 2 and 3 both made incorrect predictions).	Score 0 points.	Score 0 points.

Average Roll

- Roll a pair of dice and use the digits to form the greater 2-digit number.
- Do this 2 more times.
- Find the average of your 3 numbers to nearest whole number.
- Score 4 points for 20 or less
  - 3 points for 21 to 30
  - 2 points for 31 to 50
  - 3 points for 51 to 60
  - 4 points for 60 or greater
- Take turns. The first player to reach 30 points wins.

Example

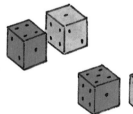

$$21 + 41 + 65 = 127$$

$$3 \overline{)127} \quad 42\frac{1}{3}$$
$$\underline{120}$$
$$7$$
$$\underline{6}$$
$$1$$

Average is 42.
Score 2 points.

Take Your Pick

THINK OF A NUMBER

Each of 20 students thinks of a number from 0 to 9. The students work in pairs. Predict how many times the sum of the partners' numbers will be less than or equal to 10. Do an experiment to check your prediction.

NAMING COINS

Eric has 5 coins. The average value of the coins is 14¢. What coins does he have?

AVERAGE DISTANCE

The average distance from school to home for Hassan, Trina, and Jean is 10 km.
Hassan lives 5 km from school and Trina lives 12 km from school.
How far does Jean live from school?

HEADS AND TAILS

Three students predicted the results of tossing two pennies. Whose prediction will likely be correct the most number of times? Explain.

1 head and 1 tail

2 heads

2 tails

CREATING NUMBERS

Two spinners are spun to get two numbers.
The numbers are multiplied.
What products are possible?
Calculate the probability of the product being 0.

Make up other problems. Post them on the bulletin board for your classmates to solve.

1. In which city would a picnic for tomorrow likely be cancelled? Explain.

St. John's – cloudy tomorrow with a 10% chance of rain

Trois Rivières – cloudy tomorrow with a 90% chance of rain

2. Which statements mean the same?
   - It is certain.
   - It is impossible.
   - The probability is 0.
   - The probability is 1.

   Give an example of an outcome with a probability
   - of 0
   - of 1

3. The average height of students in a class is 140 cm. When a new student joined the class, the average height stayed the same. How tall was the new student?

4. If the chance of winning a prize is $\frac{1}{10}$, what is the chance of not winning a prize? Explain.

5. Pick 5 numbers with an average close to 10. One of the numbers must be 20.

6. You are shown the doors to 12 rooms and told
   - in 11 rooms there is a pot of gold you can keep
   - in 1 room there is a hungry tiger

   What is the chance of finding gold? Would you take that chance? Explain.

7. What might be the missing numbers if you consider the average of the five numbers very easy to find? Explain.

   1   3   5   ?   ?

8. Calculate the probability of spinning
   - a B
   - an A

   About how many times will you spin an A in 80 tries?

9. One marble is pulled out of a bag of 100 marbles. Its color is recorded and it is returned to the bag. This is done 10 times and the results are

   How many of each color of marble are probably in the bag?

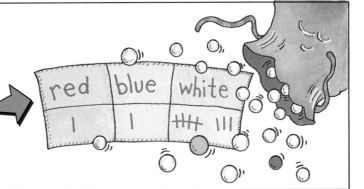

red	blue	white
l	l	ЖЖ lll

Thinking Back

Compare the chances.
What does this information tell you about buying lottery tickets?

Chances of winning the Lotto 6/49 jackpot   1 in 14 000 000

Chances of being hit by lightning   1 in 4 000 000

Is the average age of Canadians greater than your age? How do you know?

The average score on a January math test is 10. The average score on a February math test is 20. Is there enough information to tell if the students are doing better? Explain.

I get 1 point if the spinner stops on red. You get 2 points if it stops on blue.

Is this a fair game? Explain.

The size of the average Canadian family is 3.1. Explain what this means.

What questions do you still have about probability and statistics?

Investigating
Structures

About how tall is an average 10-year old?
About how tall is each building?
Compare the height of your school to the heights of these buildings.
What shapes do you see here?
in your community?

173

HOW Can Numbers Describe Tall Structures?

Empire State Building

The Empire State Building in New York City is the world's best-known skyscraper. It opened in 1931, and was for many years the world's tallest building.

Facts
381 m high
102 storeys
1860 steps
73 elevators
15 000 workers
6500 windows
600 km of power cable
elevator speed 350 m/min
about 2 million visitors/year

1. About how high is each storey of the Empire State building?
   About how many steps are there between storeys?

2. On average, about how many visitors are there each day?
   At this rate, about how long would it take for the population of Canada to visit the Empire State Building?

3. On average, about how many workers use each elevator?
   Do you think the number of elevators is reasonable? Explain.

Work with a partner.

4. The Petro-Canada Tower #2 in Calgary has 52 storeys and is 210 m high. Use this information to estimate the heights of these buildings.

Number of Storeys	
Royal Centre Tower, Vancouver	36
First Canadian Place, Toronto	72
Place Victoria, Montréal	47

Count the number of storeys in a building in your community.
Estimate the height of the building.

174

The CN Tower

The CN Tower in Toronto is the world's tallest free-standing structure, with a total height of 553 m. It was completed in 1976 and cost $52 million. The tower transmits communication signals, and is also a popular tourist centre. Each year, thousands of visitors ride in glassed-in elevators to a revolving restaurant and wide observation decks, which are 342 m above the ground.

5. The speed of the express elevators in the CN Tower is about 370 m/min.
Do you think this is faster or slower than your walking speed? a car's speed on a city street?
About how long would it take to go from the ground to the observation deck if the elevator didn't stop in between?
About how long would it take you to walk the full 553 m height of the building if it were flat on the ground?

6. On a clear day, a visitor in the CN Tower can see about 100 km away. What cities or towns could you see if you could see 100 km from your school?

7. If you were to build a scale model of the CN Tower, which of these would be a reasonable scale? Explain.
1 cm represents 1 m   1 cm represents 10 m   1 cm represents 100 m
Using the scale you chose, how high would the model be?

8. Choose the tallest structure in your community.
Compare it to the Empire State Building or CN Tower in as many ways as you can.

Did you Know...?

Brendan Keenoy climbed the 1760 steps of the CN Tower in 1989 in 7 min 52 s.

▶ About how many times faster than this is the elevator in the CN Tower?

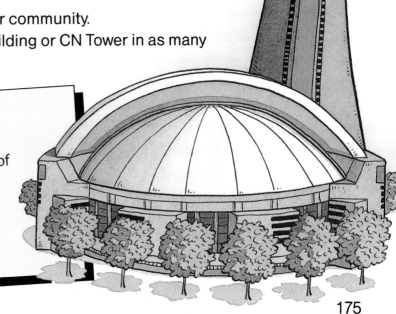

175

HOW Much Mass Can a Bridge Support?

Work in a group.

1. Make a bridge connecting the two stacks of books using an index card.
   Place a mass on the bridge. Measure the sag.

   Remove the mass and place a second card on top of the first. Put the mass back on the bridge. Now measure the sag.

   Try the same thing using three, four, and five cards. What do you notice?

   Create a graph showing the amount of sag for different numbers of cards.

2. Use four cards to build as strong a bridge as possible connecting the two stacks of books. Follow these rules:
   - The bridge must be at least 6 cm wide.
   - You may bend, fold, or cut the cards.
   - You may tape the cards to each other, but not to the books.
   - The bridge cannot touch the table. It can only touch the books.

   What is the maximum mass it can support?

3. Compare the bridges made.
   Which group has the best design?
   What makes it the best?

176

4. Make paper tubes of various lengths, distances across, and thicknesses. Test each as a bridge between two tables.

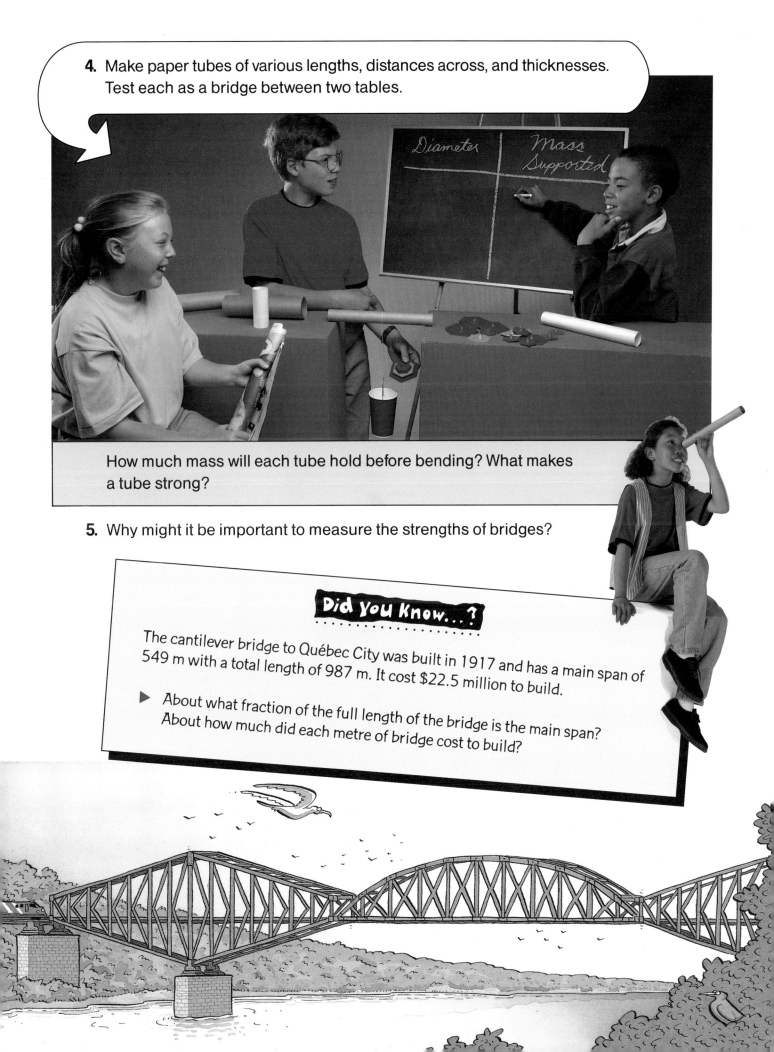

How much mass will each tube hold before bending? What makes a tube strong?

5. Why might it be important to measure the strengths of bridges?

Did You Know...?

The cantilever bridge to Québec City was built in 1917 and has a main span of 549 m with a total length of 987 m. It cost $22.5 million to build.

▶ About what fraction of the full length of the bridge is the main span? About how much did each metre of bridge cost to build?

HOW Are Simple Buildings Constructed?

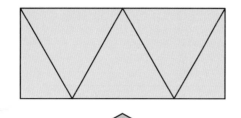

Describe the shape you expect to make, using this net.
Copy the net and make the shape.
Was your prediction right?

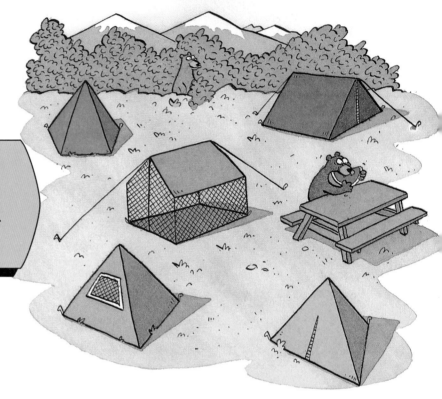

Work in a group.

1. Create a different net to make the same shape.

2. Describe the shape you
   expect to make if you connect
   toothpicks as shown and
   then connect the ends marked
   with the same letters.

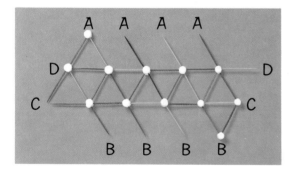

Build the shape and test
your predictions.

178

3. Cut out 20 congruent circles like this from cardboard.
Trace the triangle on each circle.

Fold along the sides of the triangle. Punch holes at the vertices.
Start connecting the folded circles together with elastics.
What shapes do you see as you connect more and more circles?
What shape do you get with 20 circles?
Have you ever seen a structure like this? What might it be used for?

Did you know...?

These houses are built with curved rather than straight sides.

▶ What shapes do these houses remind you of?
Use nets to make models of these houses. Which has the greatest floor area?
Which do you think has the greatest volume? How can you check?

Living Space

Find out and compare some floor areas of a variety of types of homes, such as a one-bedroom apartment, a two-storey house, or a bungalow.

Shoe Box Model

If a shoe box is a scale model for a building, how big would the actual building be?

Scale 1 cm represents 10 m

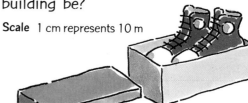

Step Climbers

Measure the height and depth of the steps on several different staircases. Try to include a spiral staircase and some outdoor staircases. Compare the measurements.
Which staircases do you find easiest to climb?
Suggest a maximum height and depth of steps that is reasonable.

Toothpick Towers

Use toothpicks and marshmallows or peas. Build the tallest structure you can. Describe what steps you took to make it strong.

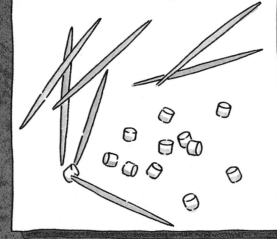

Painter's Puzzle

Estimate the number of litres of paint that would be needed to paint all the walls of your classroom.

Make up your OWN investigation. Then post it on the bulletin board for others to try.

Tell about a situation where each type of building information might be needed.
- height
- floor area
- mass
- volume
- age

How do you think the heating costs for a building relate to the floor area of the building?

Would buildings with the same floor area always have the same heating costs? Explain.

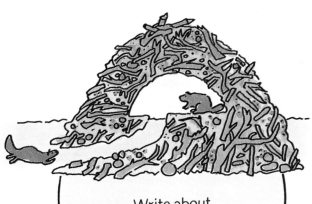

Write about some of the advantages and disadvantages of round homes.

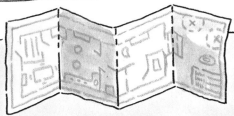

Scale models are sometimes made to show the plan of a building. Blueprints are always made. Which would you rather see if you were buying the building? if you were constructing the building? Why?

What else would you like to know about structures?
Tell what you would do to find out.

◄ These base ten blocks show 3.45.

Show
2.9   1.32   3.06

What would you have to add to the blocks in the photo to show 5?

◄ This hair has been magnified 100 times under a microscope.

What would its actual thickness be?
Why might we look at things under a microscope?

◄ A 24 g box of corn flakes contains 0.6 g of fibre. About how much fibre would be in this 400 g box?

▼ This animal has a fever.
Which animal might it be?
How much has its temperature risen?

Average Body Temperature (in °C)

Blue whale	35.5
Crocodile	25.6
Goat	39.9
Goldfish	23.5
Human	37.0

with Decimals

5.03

◀ How much will it cost for 2 tapes? 4 tapes?
How many tapes could you buy with $30?

▼ How close in length could a king cobra and a paradise tree snake be?
How far apart in length could they be?

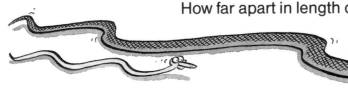

paradise tree snake — 0.9 m to 1.2 m   king cobra snake — 3.7 m to 5.5 m

▶ What might you be able
to do in 0.1 of an hour?
0.01 of an hour?

When might
you have to add
or subtract
decimal numbers?

Cheese
$4.25/kg

183

In what ways is a circle like a square?

Buying Supplies

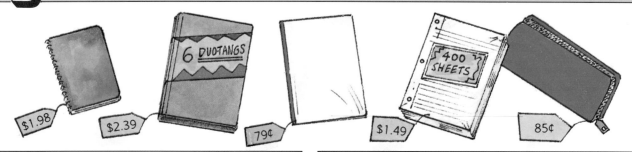

6 DUOTANGS

400 SHEETS

$1.98 $2.39   79¢ $1.49   85¢

Ron is finding the cost of a journal and a pencil case.

$2 + 85¢ is $2.85. Then take away 2¢.

Explain his thinking.

1.98
+ 0.85
2.83

Susan is finding how much more Duo-Tangs cost than looseleaf paper.

$2.39 – $1.39 is $1

Finish her work.

2.39
– 1.49

1. What is the cost of a journal and Duo-Tangs?

2. How much more do Duo-Tangs cost than a report cover?

Work with a partner.

Use play money. Record addition or subtraction sentences.

3. What is the cost of looseleaf paper and a report cover? What is the difference in their costs?

4. How many different items can you buy with $5? What change would you receive?

5. Find an item that costs about $1.50 more than another item. Exactly how much more is it?

6. Why do you think that many prices end in 9? Does this make adding and subtracting prices easy or hard? Explain.

When you find $\frac{1}{2}$, $\frac{1}{3}$, or $\frac{1}{5}$ of a number, the part is a whole number.
What could the number be?

ixing Drinks

1.36 L   355 mL

Can these drinks be mixed in a 1.5 L container?

Margot estimates.

1.360 is almost 1.4
+ 0.355 is almost 0.4
1.8   Too much

  Why does she write this?

Now she is calculating exactly how much she will have.

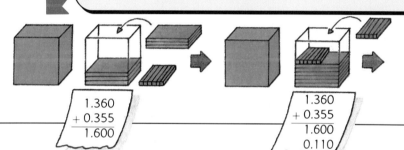

1.360
+ 0.355
1.600

1.360
+ 0.355
1.600
0.110

Why did she add 3 flats?
5 longs?
Finish her work.

Elan is mixing 1.14 L of apple juice and 295 mL of cranberry juice.

1. Estimate to see if he can use a 1.5 L container.

Elan is calculating exactly how much he will have.

ones	tenths	hundredths	thousandths

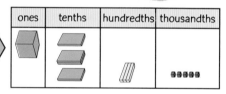

What trade did he make? Why? What will he do next? Finish his work.

1
1.140
+ 0.295
35

Work in a group.

Estimate and then calculate. Model your solutions.

1.36 L   946 mL   1.89 L   1.5 L   2.84 L   750 mL   950 mL   1.14 L   1.36 L

2. What is the least amount you can get mixing 2 of the drinks? 3 of them?

3. What is the greatest amount you can get mixing 2 of the drinks? 3 of them?

4. Can all of the drinks be mixed in a 12 L container? Explain.

What is the area of this shape?
Make 2 other shapes with 8 pegs touching the elastics and 2 pegs inside.
Find the areas. What do you notice?

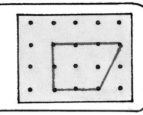

Comparing Olympic Records

Single Luge Results

	1988	1992
Men's	3:05.548	3:02.363
Women's	3:03.973	3:06.696

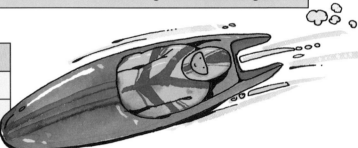

3:05.548 is read

three minutes, five and five hundred forty-eight thousandths seconds.
Read the other times.

Natalia estimates how many seconds faster the men's time was in 1992 than in 1988.

5.548 is almost   6
− 2.363 is a bit more than 2
               almost 4

Why does she write this?
Why does she ignore the 3 min?

Then she calculates.

ones	tenths	hundredths	thousandths

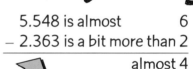

ones	tenths	hundredths	thousandths

$$\begin{array}{r} 4\;14 \\ 5.\cancel{5}\cancel{4}8 \\ -\ 2.363 \\ \hline 5 \end{array}$$

What trade did she make? Why?
What will she do next? Finish her work.

1. In which year was the women's time faster?

Estimate how many seconds faster.

Roberto is calculating how much faster by counting on.

3.973 to 3.980 is 0.007

3.980 to 4.000 is 0.020

4.000 to 6.000 is 2.000

6.000 to 6.696 is

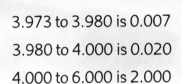

Finish his work.

Work in a group.

Estimate and then use different methods to subtract. Model your solutions.

2. In which year was the women's single luge time faster than the men's? How much faster?

3. In which year was the time faster for each skiing event? How much faster?

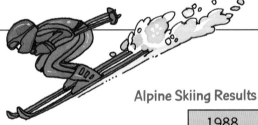

50.37 to 50.40 is 0.03

50.40 to 51.00 is

Alpine Skiing Results

	1988	1992
Men's downhill	1:59.63	1:50.37
Men's slalom	1:39.47	1:44.39
Women's downhill	1:25.86	1:52.55
Women's giant slalom	2:06.49	2:12.74

4. In which swimming event were the men's and women's winning times the closest? How close were they?

5. Why do you think decimal places to the hundredths or thousandths are used to record times? How do you think officials decide how accurate to be?

1992 Swimming Results

	Men's	Women's
100 m freestyle	0:49.02	0:54.64
100 m backstroke	0:53.98	1:00.68
100 m breast stroke	1:01.50	1:08.00
100 m butterfly	0:53.52	0:58.62

Take Your Pick

0 TO 6

Use each digit from 0 to 6 once to make this true.

```
  ?? . ??
+  ? . ??
  54 . 30
```

PREDICTIONS

Predict the numbers that will be in the seventh row.

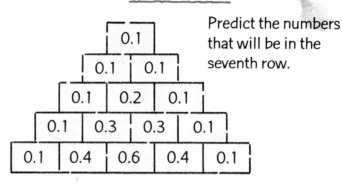

SUM AND DIFFERENCE

Luis and Elena are combining their money to buy a gift.
They have a total of $52.08.
Elena had $12.08 more than Luis.
How much did each of them have before combining their money?

MISSING TOTALS

$35.78 was spent in 4 stores.

How much might have been spent at each of Science + and Sam's?

BUYING BULK

What is the difference between the highest price and the lowest price?

Make up other problems. Post them on the bulletin board for your classmates to solve.

> Arrange 6 counters in 3 straight lines of 3 each.

Growing Bigger

. . . she opened it, and found in it a very small cake, on which the words "EAT ME" were beautifully marked in currants . . . So she set to work, and very soon finished off the cake. . . . "Curiouser and curiouser!" cried Alice . . . "Now I'm opening out like the largest telescope that ever was! Goodbye, feet!"

from *Alice in Wonderland* by Lewis Carroll

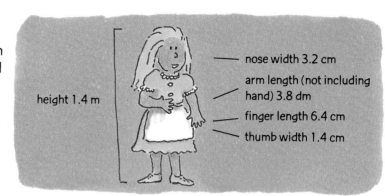

height 1.4 m

nose width 3.2 cm

arm length (not including hand) 3.8 dm

finger length 6.4 cm

thumb width 1.4 cm

> Suppose each part of Alice became 10 times as long and 10 times as wide. How wide would her thumb be?

Decimetres are 10 times centimetres. So Alice's thumb would be 1.4 dm wide.

So Alice's thumb would be 1.4 dm wide.

10 x 1.0

10 x 0.4

Work with a partner.

Who is right? Explain.

1. What would be Alice's new finger length? nose width? arm length? height?

2. Find each other's
   • height   • finger length   • thumb width   • arm length

   What would these measurement be if you ate the cake?

3. Suppose the cake made Alice 100 times as tall and wide. What would be her new finger length? nose width? arm length? height?

   How do these answers relate to those from Problem 1?

   How would they change if the cake made Alice 1000 times as tall and wide?

4.

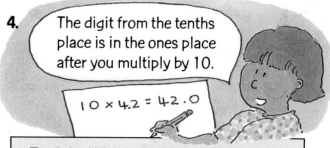

The digit from the tenths place is in the ones place after you multiply by 10.

10 × 4.2 = 42.0

Explain. Which digit would be in the ones place after you multiply by 100?

189

When a number cube is rolled

- an even number occurs about $\frac{2}{3}$ of the time

- a number greater than 10 occurs about $\frac{1}{6}$ of the time

The cube has 3 pairs of numbers each with a sum of 14. What numbers could be on the cube?

Buying Foreign Money

About how much does it cost to buy $5 U.S.?

Tara estimates.

$5 \times \$1 = \$5$ and
$5 \times 25¢ = 5$ quarters

Cost in Canadian Dollars, December 24, 1992

1 U.S. dollar	$1.26
1 British pound	$1.92
1 German mark	$0.79
1 Japanese yen	$0.01
1 French franc	$0.23
1 Irish punt	$2.09
1 Argentine peso	$1.30

Alan estimates.

$5 \times \$1 = \$5$ and
$5 \times 30¢ = 5 \times 3$ dimes
$= 15$ dimes

Why did Tara use 5 quarters?
Why did Alan use 5 groups of 3 dimes?
Finish each student's work.

1. About how much would 5 British pounds cost? 5 French francs?

2. Of which currency is Vera estimating the cost of 5 units?

3. What is the cost of $10 US?
   10 British pounds? 10 German marks?

190

Estimate and then calculate. Use play money.

4. A French franc has almost the same value as one quarter. How can you use this fact to estimate the cost of 12 francs? 25 francs? 48 francs? 58 francs? Which costs were easy to estimate? Explain why.

5. About how much Canadian money will each item cost?

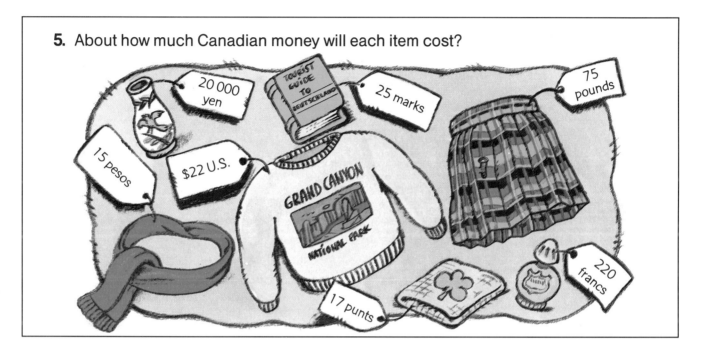

6. Why is it useful to be able to estimate the cost in Canadian dollars of items in foreign money?

7. Make up foreign money problems for these and estimate the answers.
$8 \times 0.23 \qquad 11 \times 1.92 \qquad 17 \times 1.30$

8. About how much Canadian money is each U.S. coin worth?

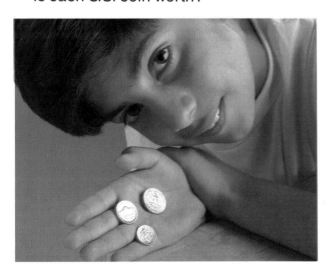

9. Foreign money exchange rates change daily. The cost of $1 U.S. was as low as $1.14 and as high as $1.29 within one year's time. Find the current exchange rates in the financial section of a newspaper.
Estimate the cost of buying 50 units of money of a country you might like to visit.

A plane leaves Toronto at 5:20 p.m. and arrives at Calgary at 7:35 p.m. How long did the flight take?

Comparing Masses of Small Animals

The royal antelope is the smallest antelope.
Its mass is about 3.3 kg.
At what age might a human have that mass?

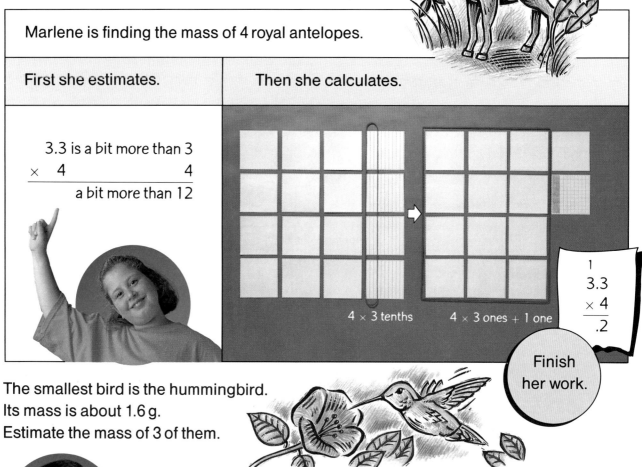

Marlene is finding the mass of 4 royal antelopes.

First she estimates.	Then she calculates.

3.3 is a bit more than 3
$$\times \quad 4 \qquad\qquad 4$$
a bit more than 12

4×3 tenths 4×3 ones + 1 one

$$\begin{array}{r} 1 \\ 3.3 \\ \times\ 4 \\ \hline .2 \end{array}$$

Finish her work.

The smallest bird is the hummingbird.
Its mass is about 1.6 g.
Estimate the mass of 3 of them.

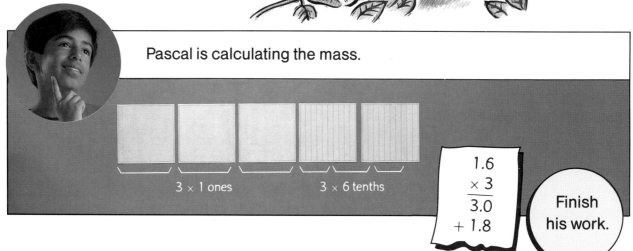

Pascal is calculating the mass.

3×1 ones 3×6 tenths

$$\begin{array}{r} 1.6 \\ \times\ 3 \\ \hline 3.0 \\ +\ 1.8 \end{array}$$

Finish his work.

192

The smallest marsupial is the long-tailed planigale. Its mass is 4.2 g.

1. What is the mass of 2 long-tailed planigales? Estimate and then calculate the mass of 5 of them. How close was your estimate? Show two ways to find the mass of 8 long-tailed planigales.

Work in a group.

Estimate and then calculate. Model your solutions. Use this information.

Smallest Animals

bumblebee bat	1.87 g
northern pygmy mouse	7.5 g
miniature chihuahua	0.63 kg
Netherland dwarf rabbit	1.02 kg
palmate newt	2.39 g

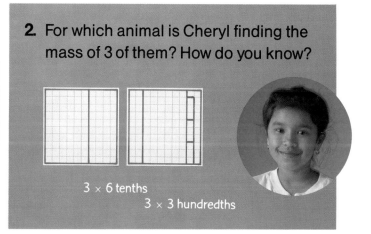

2. For which animal is Cheryl finding the mass of 3 of them? How do you know?

3×6 tenths

3×3 hundredths

3. What is the mass of each group of animals?

4. Which is heavier— 1 bumblebee bat or 3 miniature chihuahuas? Explain.

5. Which way should each of the balance scales tilt?

6. Why do you think there was no data given about the smallest insects?

ultiplying

There are lots of ways to calculate 2.56 × 8.
Here are some. Can you think of any more?

1. You could show 2.56 eight times using decimal grids.

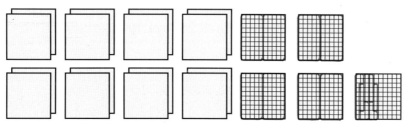

8 × 2 ones
= 16 ones

8 × 5 tenths
= 40 tenths
= 4.0 ones

8 × 6 hundredths
= 48 hundredths

8 × 2.56 – 20.48

2. You might model with money.

8 × 2 dollars = 16 dollars $16.00
8 × 5 dimes = 40 dimes   4.00
8 × 6 pennies = 48 pennies   0.48
                              $20.48

8 × 2.56 = 20.48

3. You could double 3 times.

2 × 2.56 = 5.12
2 × 5.12 = 10.24
2 × 10.24 = 20.48

8 × 2.56 = 20.48

4. You might multiply 8 and 256 hundredths.

$$
\begin{array}{r}
256 \text{ hundredths} \\
\times \quad 8 \\
\hline
2048 \text{ hundredths} = 20.48
\end{array}
$$

8 × 2.56 = 20.48

Show two different ways to do each multiplication.

1. $\begin{array}{r} 3.14 \\ \times \quad 8 \\ \hline \end{array}$ **2.** $\begin{array}{r} 5.6 \\ \times \quad 2 \\ \hline \end{array}$ **3.** $\begin{array}{r} 1.35 \\ \times \quad 4 \\ \hline \end{array}$

4. 5 × 3.321   **5.** 6 × 1.38   **6.** 9 × 0.25

DOZEN

12 pens cost exactly $12. How many of each pen were bought?

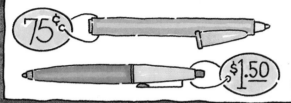

PATTERNS

Find the next three numbers in each pattern.

0.232, 2.32, 23.2, . . .

3.45, 6.90, 13.80, . . .

13.4, 26.8, 40.2, . . .

EARTHQUAKES

The Richter scale is used to measure earthquakes.
The higher the number, the stronger the earthquake.
A difference of 1.0 means an earthquake that is 10 times as strong.
A difference of 2.0 means an earthquake that is 100 times as strong.

0 1 2 3 4 5 6 7 8 9 10

How many times as strong an earthquake is 4.6 as 3.6? 7.2 as 4.2?
What earthquake would be 1000 times as strong as 3.8?

HOW MANY?

How many of each ticket could you buy with $50?
What change would you get?

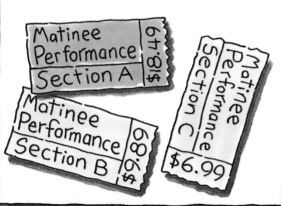

FILL IN

Fill in the digits to make this true.

$$\begin{array}{r} \boxed{?}\,2\,.\,\boxed{?} \\ \times \qquad 5 \\ \hline 2\,\boxed{?}\,1\,.\,5 \end{array}$$

Make up other problems. Post them on the bulletin board for your classmates to solve.

Find 10 ways to express 97. Use any combination of addition, subtraction, multiplication, or division.

Getting Money Back

SALE
GET BACK $\frac{1}{10}$ OF PRICE

How much money would you get back from a $10 purchase? a $1 purchase? a 10¢ purchase?

How much money is paid? given back?

Explain why this amount is given back.

PAY   GET BACK

1. Conrad spent $56.80. How many $1 coins does he get back? how many dimes? pennies? Why might you calculate 56.80 ÷ 10 to find $\frac{1}{10}$ of 56.80?

Work with a partner.

Use play money. Write division sentences.

2. How much money would you get back from a $35.90 purchase?
   Why do the amounts paid and given back have the same digits?
   Why is the ones digit in the amount paid the same as the tenths digit in the amount given back?

3. How much would you get back from each purchase?

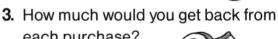

$132·70
$48·25
$30
$235·78

4. What fraction is given back here? What number would you divide by? How much would you get back from these purchases?

GET $1·00 BACK ON EVERY $100 SPENT

$200
$340
$527·20

5. What digit in the amount given back is the same as the hundreds digit in the amount paid? Explain. What about the tens digit in the amount paid?

6. How are dividing by 10 and 100 alike? different?

7. How does knowing how to multiply by 10 help you to divide by 10?

196

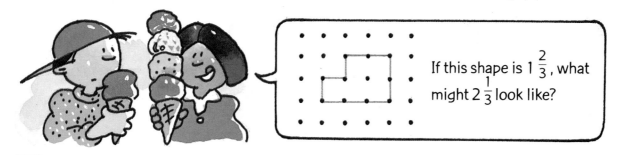

If this shape is $1\frac{2}{3}$, what might $2\frac{1}{3}$ look like?

Estimating Areas of Garbage Zones

Granby, PQ has an area of 72.6 km². If the city is divided into 5 zones for garbage pick up, estimate the average area of each zone.

Cleo estimates.

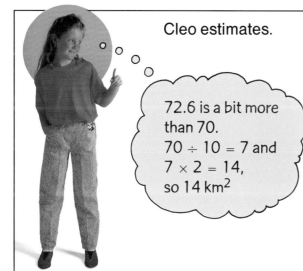

72.6 is a bit more than 70.
70 ÷ 10 = 7 and 7 × 2 = 14, so 14 km²

Why does she divide by 10 and multiply by 2?

George estimates.

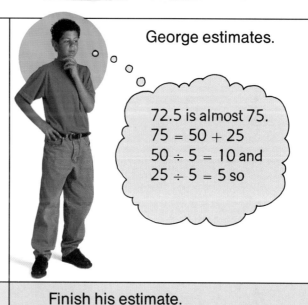

72.5 is almost 75.
75 = 50 + 25
50 ÷ 5 = 10 and 25 ÷ 5 = 5 so

Finish his estimate.
How would you have estimated?

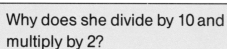

Work with a partner.

Use facts you know.

Estimate the average area if each community is divided into

1. 4 zones   **2.** 5 zones   **3.** 6 zones

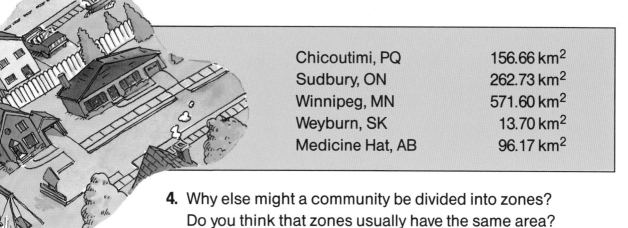

Chicoutimi, PQ	156.66 km²
Sudbury, ON	262.73 km²
Winnipeg, MN	571.60 km²
Weyburn, SK	13.70 km²
Medicine Hat, AB	96.17 km²

4. Why else might a community be divided into zones?
Do you think that zones usually have the same area?

Date	High Temperature	Low Temperature
Jan. 20	0° C	−5° C
Jan. 21	2° C	−4° C
Jan. 22	−1° C	−5° C

What is the difference between the high and low temperatures each day?

Finding the Price

Choosing a division algorithm

4 L of milk cost $3.79.
What is the price of
1 L called?

Chris finds the price of 1 L.

First he estimates.

3.79 is almost 4.
4 ÷ 4 = 1, so less than $1

Then he calculates.

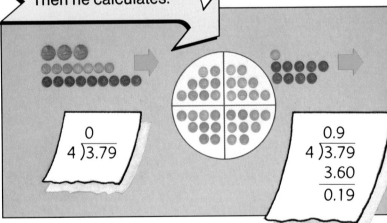

$$\begin{array}{r} 0 \\ 4\overline{)3.79} \end{array}$$

$$\begin{array}{r} 0.9 \\ 4\overline{)3.79} \\ 3.60 \\ \hline 0.19 \end{array}$$

What trade did he make?
What trade will he make next?
Finish his work.

What could you do with
the remainder?

A set of three mixing bowls costs $5.19.
Estimate the average price of one bowl.

Holly calculates.

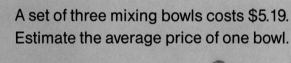

$$3\overline{)5.19}$$

$$\begin{array}{r|l} 3\overline{)5.19} & \\ 3.00 & 3 \times 1.0 \\ \hline 2.19 & \\ 2.10 & 3 \times 0.7 \end{array}$$

What trade did she make? Why?

Finish her work.

1. Would you get the same unit price as Chris if you did what Ann says? Explain.

   Would it work for finding the average price?

We found unit prices before. We changed dollars and cents to cents before we divided.

Work in a group.

Estimate and then calculate to the nearest cent. Model your solutions.

2. To find the average price of these 3 CDs, what number is divided? Find the average price.

THE DECIMAL POINTS. $18.95
$22.49
THE DIVIDERS
ELVIS AND THE SUBTRACTIONS $19.95

3. What is the unit price of each different item?

KID-TALK 6 ISSUES PER YEAR FOR $13.98

YOUNG FOLKS' ENCYCLOPEDIA $14.95 A SET

10 TARTS FOR $3.29

8 ORANGES FOR $2.59

4. Find each average price.

7 PIECE SET FOR $24.99

$10.50

THE WRONG ANSWERS $8.98

THE FIRST ADDITION

THE CORRECTIONS $9.98

$7.98

THE REMAINDERS

THE ESTIMATIONS

$8.98

Scrabble $17.50

$20.98 The Game of Life $16.98

CLUE $10.75

SCATTEGORIES JUNIOR

5. Visit a store that displays unit prices. Compare unit prices of
   • different sizes of the same brand
   • the same sizes of different brands

6. Why do we divide to find both unit price and average?

Dividing

There are lots of ways to calculate 7.38 ÷ 6.
Here are some. Can you think of any more?

---

1. You might use base ten blocks
and share among 6.

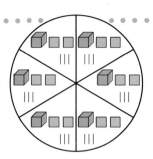

$$7.38 \div 6 = 1.23$$

---

2. You could show 7.38 on decimal grids and divide into groups of 6.

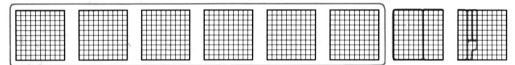

1 group of 6 ones   2 groups of 6 tenths   3 groups of 6 hundredths

              1.23 $7.38 \div 6 = 1.23$

---

3. You might rename as hundredths and rename again as numbers easy
to divide by 6.

7.38 = 738 hundredths

     = 600 hundredths + 120 hundredths + 18 hundredths

600 hundredths ÷ 6 =   100 hundredths

120 hundredths ÷ 6 =   20 hundredths

 18 hundredths ÷ 6 = $\dfrac{3 \text{ hundredths}}{123 \text{ hundredths}}$ = 1.23

                                     $7.38 \div 6 = 1.23$

---

4. You could arrange play money into
equal groups of 6.

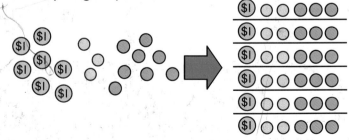

$$7.38 \div 6 = 1.23$$

Show two different ways to do
each division.

1. $9 \overline{)\, 8.88}$ **2.** $3 \overline{)\, 32.49}$

3. $7 \overline{)\, 81.6}$ **4.** 22.4 ÷ 4

5. 32.1 ÷ 5   **6.** 7.25 ÷ 8

AVERAGE PENCILS

Choose 3 pencils.
Measure each to the nearest tenth of a centimetre.
Find the average length in centimetres.
Get together with 3 others.
What is the average of your averages?

SHARING LAND

Four cousins are sharing this rectangle of land.

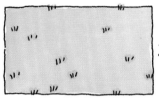

2 km

3.45 km

About how many square kilometres of land will each cousin get?

COST OF EATING

It costs, on average, $135.45 each week to feed a family of four. About how much does it cost each day to feed the family? each family member?

MOVING DIGITS

Use 2, 3, 4, 5, and 6 in different positions.

What is the greatest possible quotient? the least?
How can you get a quotient of exactly 5.89?

KEEP DIVIDING

You divide a number by 2.
You divide that quotient by 2.
You divide the last quotient by 2.
The result is 1.26.
What was the original number?

Make up other problems. Post them on the bulletin board for your classmates to solve.

201

Try this problem before going on.

NEW AVERAGE

The average of 3 numbers is 9.16. What will the average be if each number is doubled?

Ginette's group solved the problem by solving a simpler problem.

We used 3 numbers whose average was easy to find.

| Numbers | 1 | 2 | 3 | → | Average | 2 |
| Doubled | 2 | 4 | 6 | → | Average | 4 |

It looks like the average is doubled too.

We checked with 3 other easy numbers.

| Numbers | 5 | 6 | 7 | → | Average | 6 | |
| Doubled | 10 | 12 | 14 | → | Average | 12 | doubled |

The new average would be 2 × 9.16 or 18.32.

What if the numbers were tripled?

Work in a group.

Solve each problem by solving a simpler problem.

AVERAGE RAINFALL

The average monthly rainfall for 6 months was 28.5 mm. If it had rained 1 mm more each month, what would the average have been?

HOW MANY DIGITS?

How many digits would be in the product of 9 999 999 × 9 999 999?

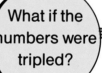

ODD LENGTHS

How much string is needed to cut lengths of 0.1 m, 0.3 m, 0.5 m, 0.7 m, 0.9 m, 1.1 m, 1.3 m, 1.5 m, 1.7 m, 1.9 m, 2.1 m, 2.3 m, 2.5 m, 2.7 m, 2.9 m?

Practising What You've Learned

Write a problem for each of these. Then solve.

1. 7.2 − 1.75

2. 5 × 1.46

3. 25.7 ÷ 100

4. 6)‾42.24‾

Solve.

5. How much would 10 stamps cost?

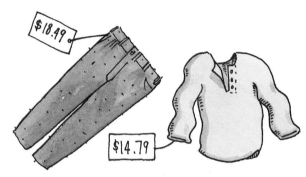

6. How much do the pants and shirt cost together?
How much more do the pants cost than the shirt?

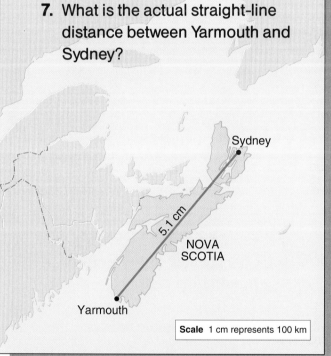

7. What is the actual straight-line distance between Yarmouth and Sydney?

Sydney

5.1 cm

NOVA SCOTIA

Yarmouth

Scale 1 cm represents 100 km

8. About how many plants could you buy with $40?

$6.29 EACH

9. 1.875 L of oil is mixed with 4.2 L of gasoline.
How much of the mixture is there?

10. What is the average length of these jumps?

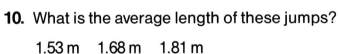

1.53 m   1.68 m   1.81 m

11. The largest camera lens is 1.372 m across. The smallest camera lens, other than for surgery and spying, is 2.9 cm across.
How many more metres across is the large lens than the small one?
About how many small lenses would fit across the large lens?

12. About 0.68 of Canadian households own a microwave oven.
About how many households would you expect to own a microwave oven in a town of 5000 households?

Playing Games for Practice

Play each game in a group of 2, 3, or 4.

Target 2.1

- Roll a die 2 times to get a 2-digit number. Use the digits in the order rolled as the ones digit and the tenths digit.
- Repeat 2 more times.
- Add or subtract any 2 of your 3 numbers trying to get as close as possible to 2.1.
- Your score is how far you are from 2.1.
- Take turns. Play 5 rounds.
- The player with the lowest score wins.

Example

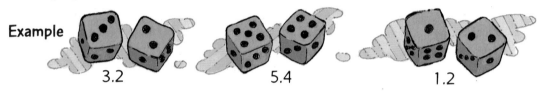

3.2   5.4   1.2

Using 3.2 and 1.2, 3.2 − 1.2 = 2.0.
Score 0.1 since 2.1 − 2.0 = 0.1.

Estimate 500

- Roll a die 3 times to get a 3-digit number. Use the digits in the order rolled as the ones digit, the tenths digit, and the hundredths digit.
- Enter your number on a calculator.
- Estimate what number to multiply it by to get as close as possible to 500. Then calculate.
- Take turns. The player with the closest estimate scores a point.
- The first player to score 10 points wins.

Example

3.65

Estimate   Multiply by 130, 4 × 130 = 520

Answer   474.5

Take Your Pick

HOW LIKELY?

If you spin the spinner twice, what is the probability of the sum being greater than 10? the difference being greater than 3?

ARRANGING DIGITS

Create a decimal number and a 1-digit whole number.
Arrange the digits to get
- the greatest quotient
- the least quotient

TRACK RECORD

The winning time for the 100 m dash in the 1992 Olympics was 9.96 s.
What would you expect the winning times to be for these distances?
200 m   400 m   800 m
Look up the records to check your predictions.

BUYING SPREE

Mike spent $28.03. What did he buy?

MYSTERY NUMBERS

If you divide a number by 4, the quotient is 1.813.
What would the quotient be if you divide the number by 2?
What is the number?

Make up other problems. Post them on the bulletin board for your classmates to solve.

1. Write an addition, a subtraction, a multiplication, and a division sentence with this answer.

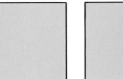

2. Tell how you could use a measuring tape to multiply 6 by 1.125.

3. Order from least to greatest without actually calculating. Tell how you did it.

$5 + 4.52$ $5 - 4.52$ 5×4.52 $5 \overline{)4.52}$

4. You multiply a number by 5 and the product is about 3. What do you know about the number?

5. How and why are the answers to these related?

5×34.2 5×3.42 342×0.5

6. Estimate the quotient of 34.2 and 7. Use the same digits — 3, 4, 2, and 7— to write a division with a quotient about 2.

7. Find two lengths that differ by 2 cm and total 6.42 cm.

8. How much is the change each time?
$2.43 from $5
$8.82 from $10

9. Find the perimeter of this rectangle.

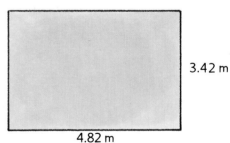

3.42 m

4.82 m

10. Four friends are sharing this giant licorice. How much does each get? How much more would each get if the licorice was 1 m longer?

3.44 m

Thinking Back

Is multiplying by 0.1 the same as dividing by 10? Why or why not?

Which operation—addition, subtraction, multiplication, or division—do you find easiest with decimals? Tell why.

Could 4.2 be the difference of two numbers with digits in the thousandths places? Explain.

Is this sum correct? Explain.

$$\begin{array}{r} 3.452 \\ +\ 1.23 \\ \hline 3.575 \end{array}$$

How are dividing decimals and dividing whole numbers alike? different?

What questions do you still have about calculating with decimals?

Examining Symmetry

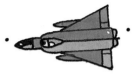

▼ Find the mistakes in the reflection.

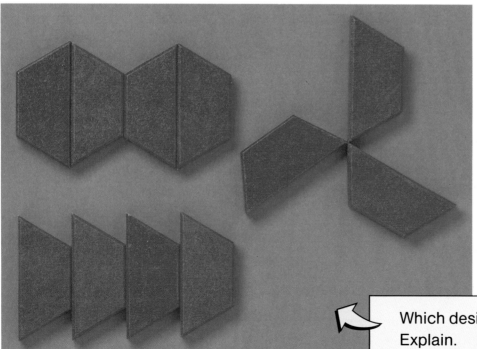

◄ Tell which design was made by sliding, flipping, or turning a trapezoid pattern block.

Which designs show symmetry? Explain.

and Motion Geometry

▼ Use any pattern block except the trapezoid.
Make a design that suggests you are sliding it.
Does your design suggest any other motions?

▲ How are the cards alike?
different?

▼ Is this octagon symmetrical? Explain.
Create a different octagon that is
not symmetrical.
Explain why it isn't.

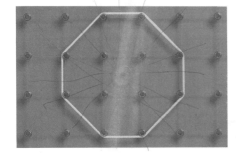

Write the word NOON
on a piece of paper.
Turn the paper upside
down.
What do you notice?
The same thing happens
to a code word for help.
What is the code word?

Examine patterns on your clothing
and the clothing of students around
you. Do any patterns suggest
slides, flips, or turns?

209

Explain Paul's thinking.

$$11 \times 34 = 340 + 34$$
$$= 374$$

Use Paul's method to
multiply 11×57 and 11×302.

Coding and Decoding Messages

Use a Mira to decode
this message.

Where did
you place
your Mira?

The Mira locates the **flip line**.
The decoded message is the **flip image** of the coded message.

1. Find the flip image of each coded
   message. Is each flip line horizontal
   or vertical?

2. How might a Mira have been used to
   code the messages ?
   Code this message.

   WAIT FOR ME

SOCCER AT 5

WE GOT A DOG

I HOPE SHE PICKS ME

LET'S TALK

3. Count the squares from the flip line to the
   • coded T   • decoded T
   • coded Y   • decoded Y

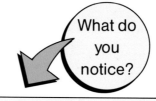

What do
you
notice?

Y S A E   S I   S I H T | T H I S   I S   E A S Y

4. Write this message on a grid.

STOP NOW

Flip it to code it.
Count the squares from the flip line to the first and
last letters in the original message.
Predict these distances for the coded message.
Check your predictions.

5. When you flip a message,
  • do any of the letters change size?
  • does the distance between
    the letters change?
  Explain.

6. Which letters in these coded messages
appear as usual? Decode the messages.

ꟽ∀⊥H ƎIЯƧ⊥

ᖴЯƎNↄH NƎX⊥

7. Where do you place a Mira so that each letter appears as usual when
coded?

A   B   C   D   E   H   I   L   M   O   S   T   Y

8. Write this message.

DOUBLE FLIP

Flip it horizontally to code it.
Then flip the coded message vertically.
What do you notice?

9. Code a message by flipping.
Give it to another group to decode.

10. June sent this message to her mom
before her mom left on a trip.
Use a Mira to decode it.
You need to place your Mira
differently for each letter.

Γ Ʌ ⊏ ⋀ Ǝ Ͷ ⊏

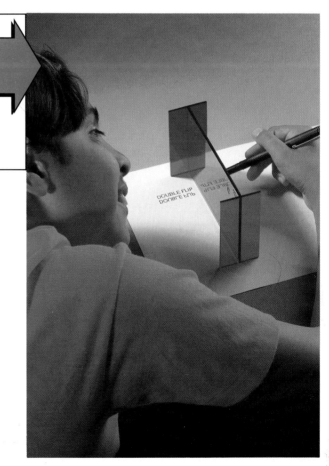

These lines are parallel.
Draw one line parallel to another.
Tell how you did it.
Could you do it another way? If so, how?

Changing Appearances

Broken sunglasses

Time to turn the hourglass over

With your book right side up,
you are viewing the picture
The tail of a fish.
Do you agree with the title?

1. Turn your book
$\frac{1}{4}$ turn clockwise.

Which picture
are you viewing now?

A diving mermaid

The tail of a fish

from *The turn about, think about, look about book*
by Beau Gardner

Turn your book another $\frac{1}{4}$ turn clockwise.
Which picture are you viewing now?
Describe how you are holding your book.

Turn your book another $\frac{1}{4}$ turn clockwise.
Which picture are you viewing?

2. What single turn from right side up lets you view *Broken sunglasses*?

212

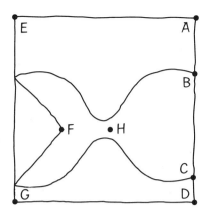

3. Trace the picture from the previous page. Label the points A to H.

4. Use A as a turn centre.
Hold your tracing down at A.
Turn your tracing $\frac{1}{4}$ turn clockwise.
What direction is the tail pointing?
Which picture is this?
Return your tracing to right side up.

5. Repeat Problem 4 for a $\frac{1}{4}$ turn clockwise at each turn centre B to H.
What did you notice about the direction of the tail?
Which turn centre moves the picture farthest to the right? to the left? up? down?

6. How far do you have to turn the picture counterclockwise to have it end up the same as a $\frac{1}{4}$ turn clockwise?

8. Create a picture that looks like something different when you turn it. Describe the amount of turn to make it look different.

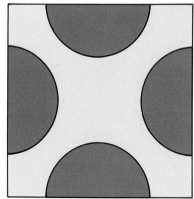

7. Why would a picture like this not be as interesting when making $\frac{1}{4}$ turns?

The surface area of one cube is 6 square units. Explain.

A structure is made by connecting 8 cubes. What is the least surface area it can have?

Capturing Treasure

Celine is close to capturing the treasure. She can use these keys or the mouse.

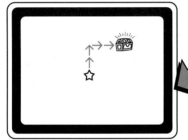

What two moves with the arrow keys will get her the treasure? Does the order of pressing the keys matter?

A single move, or slide, of the mouse ↗ would also get her the treasure.

1. Compare the direction of this slide to the slide above. What about the lengths of the slide arrows?

Work with a partner.

Use grid paper.

2. Show each move with a counter. Put a dot in the centre of each start and end square. Then draw each slide arrow as if the mouse was used.

2↑, 1→   3↑, 2→   4↑, 2→
3↑, 2←   9↑, 6→   6↑, 4←

Which slide arrows are in the same general direction? in the exact same direction? the same length?

3. You might describe this slide as very gradual up to the right.

How might you describe these slides?

214

Take Your Pick

CHESS MOVES

A knight on a chessboard can slide in these 4 ways.

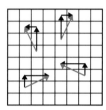

How could the knight move from A to B? A to C?

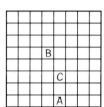

BUT HOW?

Triangle ABC was moved to the position marked as triangle DEF. Which angle corresponds to angle A? to angle B?
Which combination of slides, flips, or turns could have moved the triangle that way?

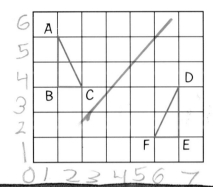

ALPHABET

Which capital letters can be turned a half turn and still look the same?
Can any be turned a quarter turn and still look the same?
What about small letters?

MIRA, MIRA

Copy this shape.

Find a way to make each design using a Mira on the shape.

COUNT THE SQUARES

Where can you place a Mira to see
10 squares?   8 squares?
6 squares?   7 squares?

Make up other problems. Post them on the bulletin board for your classmates to solve.

215

Are there more multiples of 7 between 548 and 650 or between 748 and 850?
Tell why.

Making Traffic Signs

Creating shapes with line symmetry

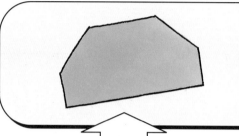

You can make a symmetric sign by folding a piece of paper and cutting out half of the shape around the fold.

What traffic sign will this look like when it is unfolded?

How can you check without making it?

Why will it be symmetric?

The fold line is called the **line of symmetry**. Why?

Work in a group.

Use paper, scissors, and a Mira.

1. Which of these signs can be made by folding a piece of paper and cutting half the shape? Make them.

 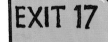

Which signs could have been made by folding in a different place?
How many lines of symmetry do they have?

2. Some signs can be made using a double fold.
Predict what shape these will be when they are cut out and unfolded.

Make them to test your predictions.
How many lines of symmetry do they have?

3. Which of these signs could be made using a double fold? Explain.

4. How can you use flips to determine whether a shape has line symmetry?

You can only travel on grid lines. Find a point that is twice as far from (2, 3) as from (5, 4). Is there more than one?

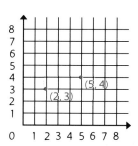

Turning Fasteners

Draw what the screw nail would look like after it is turned

- a $\frac{1}{4}$ turn
- a $\frac{1}{2}$ turn
- a $\frac{3}{4}$ turn
- a full turn

Which turns look alike?

1. What fraction of a full turn could this screw nail be turned so that it looks like it hasn't been turned at all?

2. Both of the screw nails have turn symmetry. Why?

 **Use nuts, washers, and screw nails. Turn those you have. Predict for the others.**

3. What is the least fraction of a full turn you could turn each nut or washer to show that it has turn symmetry?

4. Which of these screw nails have the same turn symmetry? Explain.

5. What would each screw nail look like after $1\frac{1}{2}$ turns?

   How does knowing the turn symmetry of each help you predict?

6. Why do you think screw nails, washers, and nuts have turn symmetry?

217

The average high temperature for a week was 1°C. What might the high temperature have been each day if Monday was 3°C?

Finding Symmetry in Art

Comparing line and turn symmetry

Many art patterns have symmetry. What symmetry do you see in this pattern?

 Use tracing paper.

1. Trace each pattern.
Fold the tracing to find lines of symmetry. Turn the tracing to find the least fraction of a full turn for it to match its picture.

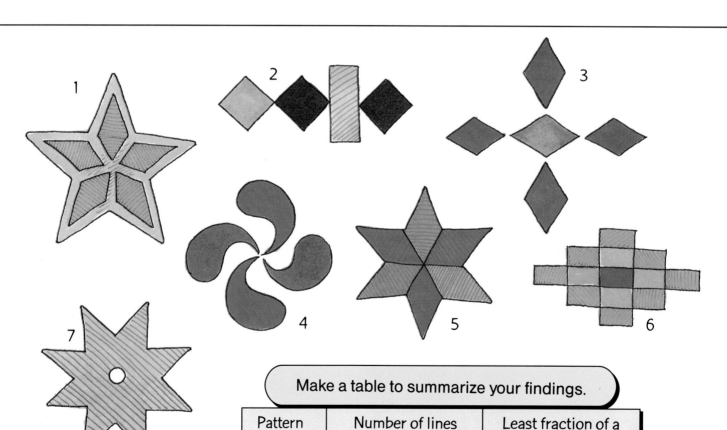

Make a table to summarize your findings.

Pattern	Number of lines of symmetry	Least fraction of a turn to match
1	?	?
2	?	?

2. Which pattern has the most lines of symmetry?
Which can be turned the most ways to match its picture?

3. A pattern that needs a full turn to match its picture does not have turn symmetry. Why do you think that is?

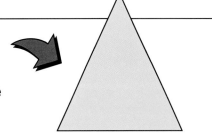

4. This triangle has exactly the same symmetry as pattern 2. Why?
Draw a shape with exactly the same symmetry as another art pattern.

5. Use the art pattern with just line symmetry.
Alter it so that it has turn symmetry.
Explain how you did it.

6. Use the art pattern with just turn symmetry.
Alter it so that it has line symmetry.
Explain how you did it.

7. Design a pattern for another group to describe the symmetry.

8. Some people believe that animals have line symmetry because they move and they need protection on both sides. Plants tend to have turn symmetry because of their need for light.
Describe the symmetry you see in animals.
Find plants or pictures of plants that have turn symmetry.

219

TURN A GEOBOARD

What is the least fraction of a full turn you could turn this geoboard for the shape to look the same?

Make 3 other shapes on a geoboard with the same turn symmetry.

CANDLES

The 5 candles on this cake form 2 lines of symmetry.

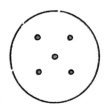

Draw the top of a cake with 13 candles and
• 2 lines of symmetry
• 3 lines of symmetry
• 4 lines of symmetry

FOUR PIECES

Trace the shapes. Put them together to make a shape with line symmetry.

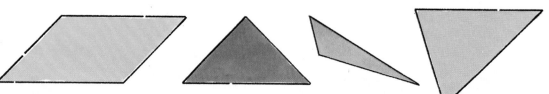

Make your own puzzle like this one for someone else to solve.

DESIGN A PLATE

What type of symmetry does this plate have?

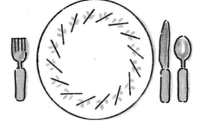

Design a border pattern for a plate so that it has both turn and line symmetry.

ALTERATIONS

Use each shape to create a new shape that still has turn symmetry.

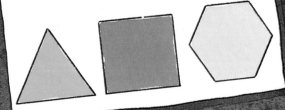

Make up other problems. Post them on the bulletin board for your classmates to solve.

Solving a Problem by Finding and Extending a Pattern

Try this problem before going on.

MYSTERY SYMBOLS

Extend this pattern.

Nathan's group solved this problem by finding a pattern.

Each symbol is symmetric.
We drew the lines of symmetry.

The parts to the right of the lines are the numbers 3, 6, 9, and 12.
These are multiples of 3.
Then we continued the pattern.

What is the twelfth symbol in this pattern?

Work in a group.

Solve these problems by finding and extending a pattern.

HIEROGLYPHICS

Explain this pattern.
What are the next 5 designs?

EMS

Continue the pattern with 2 more designs. How many M's are in the 8th design?

ANGLES

The first diagram shows ∠BAD.
Inside it are two other angles, ∠BAC and ∠DAC.
There are three angles altogether.
How many angles are in the second diagram?
Continue the pattern until you can determine how many angles will be in the 8th diagram.

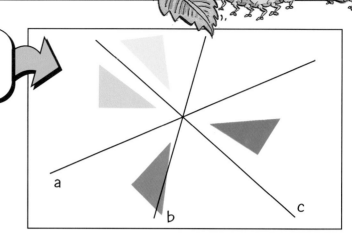

1. Which flip line goes with which flip image of the green triangle? Why?

2. Suppose the letter F is turned a quarter turn clockwise about the point. Draw what it would look like.

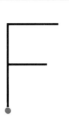

3. Which of these are not slide images of the red triangle? Explain.

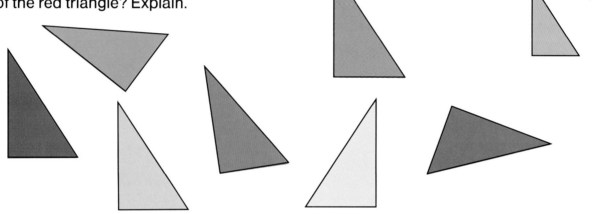

4. How many ways will each lid fit on its box?

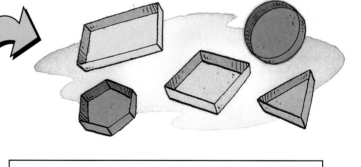

5. Look at the back of your textbook. What type of symmetry does the logo have?

6. Make a shape with line symmetry using

   • pattern blocks
   • a Mira
   • folding and cutting

   Do any of your shapes have turn symmetry?

7. Finish each design so it will have line symmetry.

8. Draw two different shapes that have exactly the same line and turn symmetry.

Play each game in a group of 2, 3, or 4.

Point Plot

- Each player labels a 6 by 6 coordinate grid using the colors of the dice that will be used.
- Take turns rolling the dice to get an ordered pair.
- Plot that point.
- The first player who can create a shape with symmetry by joining 3 or more plotted points wins the round.
- Play 5 rounds.

Example

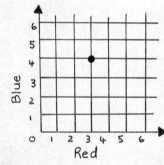

Slide, Flip, and Turn

- Each player colors half a square to form a triangle in the top left square of a 5 by 10 grid.
- Take turns spinning the spinner.
- Follow the directions to decide where to move.
- Move your triangle if possible.
- The first player to get to the bottom right square wins.

Example

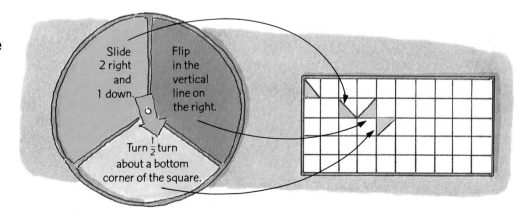

Take Your Pick

HINGED MIRRORS

Set up two mirrors taped together.
Put a square in the corner between the mirrors.
Describe what you see.

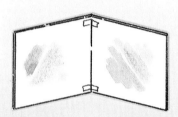

Set up the mirrors so that a similar thing happens when you put a triangle in the corner between the mirrors. What do you see?

TURN TO SLIDE

Think about how you might move a heavy piece of furniture by yourself.
Then show or tell how two turns could have the same result as a slide.

ARROWS

If you use a Mira to flip this arrow, which of these situations might you see?

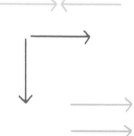

DIGITS

Examine the digits.
Describe the symmetry of each.

SYMMETRY—MORE OR LESS

Can one shape have more lines of symmetry than another, but turn to match itself in fewer ways?
Explain.

Make up other problems. Post them on the bulletin board for your classmates to solve.

1. How do you know that the blue triangle cannot be the flip image of the red one?

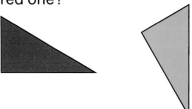

2. What motions does this strip pattern show?

Create a strip pattern that shows slides and turns.

3. Trace this diagram. Then draw slide arrows to connect vertices of the yellow kite with the matching ones of the green kite.
   What do you notice about the slide arrows?
   What solid shape does your diagram look like?

4. Describe the symmetry in each shape.

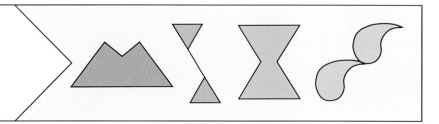

5. Can a trapezoid have line symmetry? turn symmetry? Explain or show.

6. How much farther from the flip line is D than E?

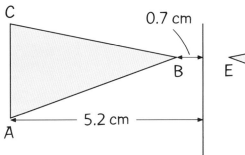

7. Create a unique shape that has 4 lines of symmetry.

8. Do any parallelograms have line symmetry? Explain.

Thinking Back

Why is it often difficult to tell a reflection from the real thing? What could make it easier?

Can you tell whether a slide, flip, or turn has been performed when you look at the shapes on the left? on the right? Explain.

Write a paragraph describing what it would be like if you weren't symmetric.

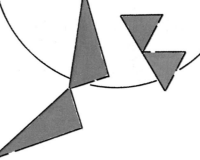

How are line symmetry and turn symmetry different?

Tell something that is true about turns and flips, but not true about slides.

What questions do you still have about symmetry and motion geometry?

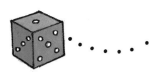 

UNIT
13

Investigating Games

The Great Car Race

- Place 12 cars (counters) on the START line.
- Toss 2 dice and find the sum.
- Move the car with that number one space forward.
- Continue until one car reaches the FINISH line.

Does this seem like a fair game? Explain.

Predict which car number would win most often.

Play the game several times.

Keep a record of each winning car number.

How good was your prediction?

What games do you like to play? Which do you play the best?

HOW Can We Predict Divisibility?

Zero Remainder

- Choose and record any divisor from 2 to 9.
- Roll 3 dice. If you do not get 3 different numbers, continue until you do.
- Write all the 3-digit numbers possible.
- Divide each 3-digit number by your divisor.
- Score 1 point each time you have 0 remainder.
- Take turns rolling the dice.
- Continue to play until one player has 20 points.

How many 3-digit numbers are possible in each round?

What are they for this round?

Find each player's score for this round.

Work in a group.

1. Play Zero Remainder. Record the divisors chosen and the digits rolled. Save all your calculations to help you answer the rest of the questions.

2. Which divisor scored the most points altogether?

Divisor	Digits	Score
3	1,2,4	0
4	1,2,4	2
6	1,2,4	0

3. Which two divisors always scored either 0 or 6 points?
   Add the 3 digits rolled each time. What do you notice? Describe numbers that can be divided evenly by each of these two divisors.

4. Was 5 a good divisor for scoring? Why or why not?
   What other digit could numbers end in and be divided evenly by 5?

5. Numbers that can be divided evenly by a number are said to be **divisible** by that number.
   Describe numbers divisible by 5.

6. Examine the last digit of each number divided evenly by 2. Describe numbers divisible by 2.

7. Examine the last two digits of the numbers divided evenly by 4. Describe numbers divisible by 4.

8. Your divisor is 2. No matter what the last die shows, how many points can you be sure of? Why?
   What would you prefer the last die to show?

9. Your divisor is 2 and the dice show 3 odd numbers. How many points will you score? Why?
   What other divisors would definitely score the same number of points? Why?

10. This was rolled. You score 6 points. What could your divisor be?

11. If a number is divisible by 2 and by 3, then it is divisible by 6.
    Do you agree or not?
    Explain why.

Did You Know...?

Dominoes is an ancient game. A standard pack is called Double 6 because the highest domino has 6 dots in each half. Here are all the dominoes with 0 dots in one half.

▶ List or draw the 28 dominoes in a standard pack. How many dominoes would there be in a pack called Double 8?

How Can Shapes Be Arranged on a Gameboard?

The Last Triomino

- Take turns coloring a triomino on a 5 × 5 gameboard.
- No triominoes can overlap.
- Continue until no more triominoes can be colored.
- The winner is the player who colors the last triomino.

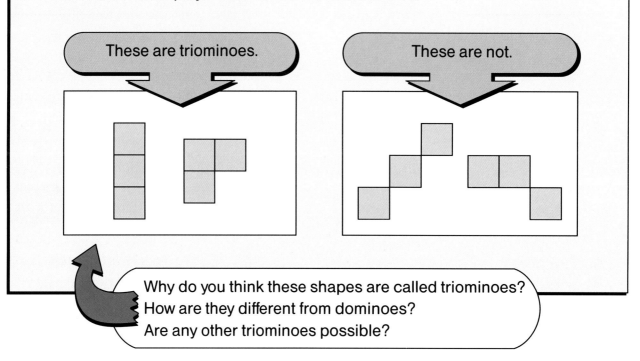

These are triominoes.

These are not.

Why do you think these shapes are called triominoes?
How are they different from dominoes?
Are any other triominoes possible?

1. You are blue and it's your turn. Describe where to color a triomino to ensure that you will win.

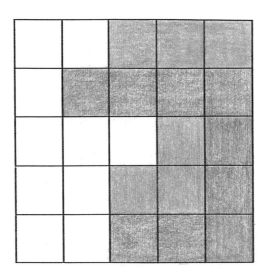

2. Use the motions slide, flip, and turn to describe pairs of triominoes.

If you flip the yellow triomino, you get the purple one.

230

3. Play The Last Triomino several times before answering the rest of the questions.
Keep track of who goes first and who wins.

4. Is it possible to fill all squares on the gameboard? Explain.

5. What sizes of square gameboards could be completely filled if only one shape of triomino was used in a game?

6. Use each motion once to describe a different pair of triominoes in one of your games.

7. What fraction of the games did the player who went first win? second? Do you think it's better to go first or second in this game?

8. Play this variation of The Last Triomino several times using each shape.

Variation: Each triomino colored must be a slide image of the previous one. Keep track of who goes first and who wins.

9. Is it better to go first or second when playing the variation?

10. These are tetrominoes. There are three others. What are they?

Make up and play a game using tetrominoes. What size of gameboard did you use?

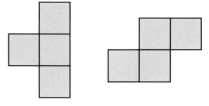

Did you know...?

The slowest game of competitive chess ended in a tie and took 15 h to play 56 moves.

▶ About how long did each move take?

HOW Much Money Will Be Won?

Money Path– A Game of Chance

- Place a penny on START.
- Toss another penny twice.
- Each time it lands heads, move the marker penny 1 space to the right.
- Each time it lands tails, move the marker penny 1 space up.

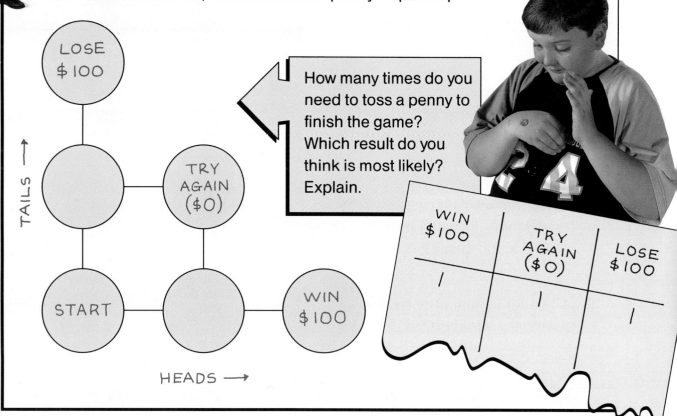

How many times do you need to toss a penny to finish the game? Which result do you think is most likely? Explain.

WIN $100	TRY AGAIN ($0)	LOSE $100
I	I	I

Work in a group.

Compare your results with other groups.

1. Play Money Path 8 times as a group, taking turns tossing and moving the pennies. Tally the results. How good was your prediction?

2. After what combinations of tosses did you land on TRY AGAIN?   WIN $100?

3. Make a bar graph to show the number of times each result happened.

4. Find the average amount of money won or lost.

5. For this gameboard, how many times do you need to toss a penny to finish the game?
How would you complete this gameboard so that you are most likely to break even?

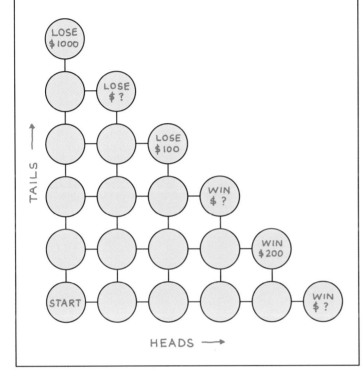

TAILS →

LOSE $1000

LOSE $?

LOSE $100

WIN $?

WIN $200

START

WIN $?

HEADS →

6. After what combinations of tosses would you land on LOSE $1000? LOSE $100? WIN $200?

7. Play this variation of Money Path 32 times. Tally and then graph the results.
Compare the shape of this graph to the shape of your first graph.
Find the average amount of money won or lost.

8. How would you rearrange the results on the gameboard so that you are more likely to win money than lose it?
Play your variation of Money Path and check.

9. Design a similar game using a different number of spaces and different results.
Tell whether you are more likely to win or lose money.
Play your game and check.

Did you know...?

On an average day, Canadians spend $958 904 buying video games. Of this total, $767 123 is spent on Nintendo games.

▶ In one week, about how much do Canadians spend buying video games that are not Nintendo games? Make up two other questions that use this information.

Predicting Sums

Shuffle nine cards. Then place them face down in a row in front of a group of 3 or 4. Before a pair of cards is turned face up, ask each student to predict whether the sum of the two numbers will be

- 7 or less
- 8 to 12
- 13 or greater

Repeat the entire process several times and keep a tally of the sums that occur. Which sums occur most frequently? Tell how you could make this into a game.

Paper, Rock, and Scissors

Flash one of these hand signs at the same time as a friend.

paper   rock   scissors

Keep a tally of wins, losses, and ties using this scoring system.

Paper covers rock.   Rock dulls scissors.   Scissors cut paper.

Play the game 20 times. What is the probability that you will both show the same hand sign so that no one wins a game?

Tic-Tac-Toe

How many different ways are there to win at Tic-Tac-Toe?
Play several games. Do players win more often when they start first? when they place their mark in the centre?

Renting Versus Buying

Find and compare the costs of renting and buying a popular video game.
How many times would you have to rent the game before it costs more than buying?

Make up your OWN investigation. Then post it on the bulletin board for others to try.

The wheel is spun twice to get two numbers.
If the difference between the numbers is less than 8, I win.
If not, you win.

Explain why you wouldn't play this game.

According to experts, the first 4 moves in a chess game can be played in 197 299 ways!
Tell what you could do to estimate how long it would take a player to try every possible move.

Some magazines use numbers from 0 to 10 to rate video games where 0 means poor and 10 means excellent.
One game scored Graphics: 9
Sound: 10
Challenge: 10
Average Rating: 9.67
Ask several students to rate different video games. Then tell how averages can be used to rate games.

Find a game that uses math.
Show a group of students how to play it.

What else would you like to know about games?
Tell what you would do to find out.

Index

236